Adv_____ _____ _____ _____ _____ _____ess _uccess

"This is the ___ ___ ___ ___ ___ ___ teacher would like you to commit to memory. Read it before you type something that could get you fired." —Alisa Bowman, journalist and coauthor of *Pitch Perfect*

"Sandra E. Lamb has made an enviable career out of practicing what she preaches. Her latest book, *Writing Well for Business Success*, will benefit anyone who's trying to make the great leap from academic writing (often stuffy, wordy, and riddled with jargon) to clear and concise professional writing." —Richard Nordquist, professor emeritus of English and author of the guide to grammar and composition at About.com

"Sandra Lamb is a pro's pro as a writer, editor, and coach. Her book is an important resource for anyone interested in clear, concise communications in the business world." —Timothy Harper, editor and publisher of *CUNY Journalism Press* and writing coach of the CUNY Graduate School of Journalism

"Yes, it's possible to write business prose without sounding like Mr. Burns. Sandra Lamb can tell you how to deliver that bad-news memo, how to write emails like a grown-up, how to take blame without groveling, and how to be grammatically correct without being stiff. She knows! And anyone who advises against 'repurpose' and 'strategic fit' gets my vote." —Patricia T. O'Conner, author of *Woe Is I* and, with Stewart Kellerman, *Origins of the Specious*

"Everybody complains about poor nonfiction writing, but Sandra Lamb is doing something about it. Businesses that assign her sensible and useful new book on writing may start to save some of the billions of dollars now being poured into remedial writing classes for all levels of employees." —Will Fitzhugh, *The Concord Review*

WRITING WELL

for

BUSINESS SUCCESS

A COMPLETE GUIDE
TO STYLE, GRAMMAR,
AND USAGE AT WORK

SANDRA E. LAMB

ST. MARTIN'S GRIFFIN ◆ NEW YORK

www.stmartins.com

Illustrations copyright © 2015 by J. M. Jensen

Grateful acknowledgment is made for permission to reproduce from the following:

Corporate correspondence and biography of Ginni Rometty courtesy of International Business Machines Corporation. Copyright © 2014 International Business Machines Corporation.

The Library of Congress Cataloging-in-Publication Data is available upon request.

ISBN 978-1-250-06451-6 (trade paperback)
ISBN 978-1-4668-9041-1 (e-book)

St. Martin's Griffin books may be purchased for educational, business, or promotional use. For information on bulk purchases, please contact the Macmillan Corporate and Premium Sales Department at 1-800-221-7945, extension 5442, or write to specialmarkets@macmillan.com.

First Edition: August 2015

10 9 8 7 6 5 4 3 2 1

For Charles, whose words remain

Contents

Acknowledgments ix
Preface xi
Introduction 1

═══════════ **PART ONE** ═══════════

FIRST THINGS FIRST

1	Before You Write	5
2	Create a Road Map	13
3	What's Your Point?... and Other Principles	18
4	Write, Write, Write	31
5	Revise, Revise, Revise	45
6	Edit, Edit, Edit	48

═══════════ **PART TWO** ═══════════

PERFECT WHAT YOU'VE WRITTEN

7	Write with Style, Voice, and Tone	69
8	Punctuation Slam Dunks	73
9	Caution: Yield to Grammar and Usage—*or Not!*	86
10	Misused, Confused, and Abused Words	106
11	Business Writing Etiquette	126

===== **PART THREE** =====

THE SHAPES OF
BUSINESS COMMUNICATIONS

12 The Email Animal
    (and All Its Electronic Relatives)   137

13 Memos That Make the Point   152

14 Letters That Hit the Mark   158

15 The Business Plan That Gets Action   183

16 The Report That Changes Things   190

17 Proposals and Grant Applications
    That Get Approved   203

18 The Presentation That Gets the Contract   212

19 The Speech That Gets Applause   218

20 The Résumé That Gets the Interview   222

References   243
Index   245

Acknowledgments

Certainly heaps of gratitude are owed to those pioneers of punctuation, grammar, and usage rules who penned the bedrock guiding epistles, and I'm equally indebted to all those hard-bitten editors of my early professional efforts who unfailingly red-flagged my errant prose—KO'ing superfluous commas, undithering run-on sentences, and eliminating useless or standard phrases. There were many.

Without the muddled reports, bewildering proposals, inscrutable résumés, and fractured emails that have littered my inbox over the years, or have come through the mail—and certainly the abundant number I've written—I would not have been inspired to write this book. So thanks to all those unwitting scribes, as well.

A special thanks to the gaggle of librarians who were eager to help and for their relentless work on my behalf; especially, thanks to Joe Cahn, brilliant reference librarian at the Denver Public Library, for his repeated and tireless digging for that yet-one-more example or remote reference source.

Thanks to my husband, Charles, who encouraged me to begin this project but didn't live to see this book finished.

And, finally, thanks to the great St. Martin's Press team for their patience and perseverance in getting this book over the finish line. The errors that remain are mine alone.

Preface

You may be saying, "Really? Another book on writing?"

And you'd be right. We have oodles of books on the art of bending a verb and inserting—or not inserting—a comma. Everyone, it seems, has taken up the mantle, starting with classics you were first assigned in English 101 A: *The Elements of Style*—by William Strunk, Jr., and his subsequently credited student cum editor and coauthor, E. B. White—and *On Writing Well* from that other William, William Zinsser.

We have hordes of books on grammar, style, punctuation, and structure. To make these nuts-and-bolts tomes more inviting, some were given exotic titles designed to intrigue or make the whole topic seem a bit sexier, like Constance Hale's *Sin and Syntax*, Bill Walsh's *Lapsing Into a Comma*, or Karen Elizabeth Gordon's *The Deluxe Transitive Vampire*. To appeal to the intellectual audience, some academic authors have given their books titles like Steven Pinker's *The Sense of Style: The Thinking Person's Guide to Writing in the 21st Century*.

Then there are the fed-up editors of time-honored bastions of properly punctuated and phrased newspaper prose, like Patricia O'Conner, William Safire, and Bill Walsh, who've each tried to correct the errant ways of the pedestrian nonfiction writer who is challenged to match a singular subject with a compatible verb.

Add, of course, those creative-arts varieties aimed at helping you hone the skills of wordsmithing that novel that lies deep within your subconscious. These books have been written by some of the famed masters of creative writing over the ages, and include titles like Eudora Welty's *On Writing* and Stephen King's book with the same title. That names just two.

So why another book on writing? *Writing Well for Business Success* enters this hallowed and well-populated territory with one express purpose: to help the business writer master the skills of effective business writing in the fast-paced world of electronic business transmissions. A daunting task? Not really. It can be accomplished by employing and practicing the simple principles and tips within these pages. Writing well can mean the difference between getting that coveted job and not getting it, being promoted and being passed over. And, above all, writing well in business will not only bring you accolades from colleagues and competitors but will also save you time, give you confidence, and bring you great joy and pleasure!

WRITING WELL

for

BUSINESS SUCCESS

Introduction

When attendees at an ongoing business writing seminar were asked, "How many of you receive badly written emails?" every person raised a hand. Eyes rolled.

The complaints that tumbled out were:

► Emails with run-on sentences
► Emails that ramble and are unclear
► Punctuation and grammatical errors
► A tone that is offensive or annoying
► Improper use of the subject line
► Careless or improper use of REPLY ALL, FORWARD, TO, CC, and BCC
► Improper, brusque, or no greeting
► Ignorance of organization email protocol and political correctness

We started that day, right there, to help those attendees write emails that work. And hopefully, that's what this little book will do for you.

Writing Well for Business Success combines the best principles of William Strunk, Jr., and E. B. White's *The Elements of Style* and William Zinsser's *On Writing Well* into one concise and up-to-the-minute little volume that can become your quick-reference bible on effective business writing for today's workplace. And it includes the latest skills needed to effectively use today's number one business communications vehicle—email.

Maybe it's been a while since you stepped out of that English 101 classroom where *The Elements of Style* was taught and *On Writing Well* was required reading. And perhaps the rules for whether the word should be *that* or *which,* and whether you should use a comma or not, are a bit fuzzy. Still, you know one thing for certain: *to succeed in business you must write well* because learning to write effectively can:

- ▶ Save you—the business writer—time
- ▶ Advance your career
- ▶ Save your organization money—and lots of it
- ▶ Make your organization, and you, much more profitable
- ▶ Raise the tide of well-written business communications
- ▶ Improve everyone's disposition

But business owners are reporting that while writing well is the most essential skill for business success, it is still their employees' biggest challenge—both for those just entering the business world and for those who have been in the workforce for some time. The problems for the two groups may be different, but both groups need help.

The pervasive use of email for business has made the work of writing well even more difficult because it invites—relentlessly—hitting SEND before you have done the preliminary steps of thinking through, organizing, reviewing, and possibly rewriting your message. And before you have done the essential job of editing, editing, editing.

So, to help you get these steps done at the speed of business email today, this little book is designed as your at-the-ready reference. You'll find the steps and rules set out so they are quick to read and easy to grasp and follow. Even fun. And each step and rule given is reinforced with examples to bring the principles home.

Let's get started.

First, peruse the brief chapters to learn where to go for answers to the things you struggle with.

Then do a quick review of the chapters on email, reports, business plans, letters, presentations, and résumés. This will give you a good idea of where to turn when you have a question or need a refresher.

FIRST THINGS FIRST

I recently conducted a workshop for middle managers that was aimed at helping them improve their email writing skills. To start, I asked, "How many of you receive far too many emails that add no value and waste your time?" Every person raised a hand. "So," I continued, "would you say the *first* problem in business emails is the writer's failure to determine if he has something of value to say?" Heads nodded.

Comments from the audience that followed focused on two major email time-wasters: the "me too" messages in response to group emails that require everyone's time and add no value, and the colleague who hits REPLY ALL when he wants to communicate with one person in the email group.

As the next step, I wanted to find out if these managers recognized badly written emails when they read them. I asked, "How many of you receive emails each day that you don't understand?" Again, hands shot up, eyes rolled, and a murmur washed across the room. The managers agreed it was a daily problem.

"What is the biggest problem with these emails?" I asked.

One manager shouted, "Lack of organization." There were nods and murmurs of agreement.

"Do you mean that the messages are disorganized?" I asked.

"Yes," came the quick answer, and more nods of agreement from across the room.

"OK, what would you list as the next most frequent problem with the emails you receive?"

Shouts, like popcorn kernels exploding, went off: "Not relevant," "Not understandable," "Lack of simplicity," "Lack of clarity," "Bad grammar," "Offensive tone," "Redundant," and "Lack of editing." Again, most in the audience agreed with each of these assessments as I listed them on the board.

After more discussion, I summarized by asking: "So, would you conclude that for you to write an effective email that is sure to get read and understood, you need to (1) think through what you want to write and determine if you have something of value to say; (2) determine who you are writing to, and what he knows about the subject, so you can aim your message to make it relevant; (3) know what you want your audience to do after reading your message, so you can build it correctly; (4) organize your message in the most logical way; (5) use language that is easy to understand and invites the reader to read it; (6) use words that make your message as simple and clear as possible; and (7) edit your message to its most concise form?" While I listed these points, I wrote them on the board opposite the first list.

Each person in the audience slowly signaled agreement that taking these steps would mean that they could write effective business emails.

But then, one by one, the managers asked that I review each of these steps because—they agreed—their success in business depends on being able to write effective emails. And quickly. And, they also agreed, they could all use at least a little help to make that happen.

1

Before You Write

William Zinsser, in his classic book *On Writing Well,* points out that business writing needs to "convey the rhythms of human speech," using words that "have air around them." I'd say that means to write like you speak—in as few words as possible—and use action verbs to carry water. This will invite the reader to read; it will draw a straight line from what you want to convey to the reader's reaction to your words. And in the process, it will save everyone time and effort.

That doesn't mean you don't need to give forethought and planning to what you'll write. Look over the seven steps listed under "First Things First." Yes, even in the heat of workplace pressures that compel you to respond to that email instantly and to complete that report almost as quickly, these steps will help you create an effective, successful business communication.

Practicing these steps will help you make effective writing a habit. As you continue to use them, you'll begin to change your thinking patterns until the steps become automatic.

Conversely, if you don't do these steps of initial hard thinking, you may be like the driver in a foreign country without a GPS, a map, or a guide. Your message will wander, get lost, and never get the result you want. And not taking these steps will announce to your audience that you lack the writing skill that is essential for you to succeed in business.

ADD VALUE

Adding value to a group email thread comes down to having something new and beneficial to say. Far too many business emails fail here. There is always the temptation to add a "me too" message, which usually takes the form of "I agree with Tim on this." Resist the temptation. Unless consensus is being sought or a vote is being taken, don't fill your colleagues' inboxes with chaff. If you originate a group email, you can help eliminate unnecessary emails by directing your colleagues to weigh in *only* if they disagree or have new information to add.

FOCUS ON YOUR READER

When you know what you want to communicate, ask yourself: *Who is my audience, and what does he know about the subject?* This will give you the correct framework to start developing your message. *Who* is where you should begin; even picture him (them) in your mind, if possible. Once you can name him, ask the next question: *What* does he know about the subject? If you are writing a progress report on the organization's research and development (R & D) program, for example, what you include in the report that is aimed at the team doing the work will be very different from the report you write for your board of directors. Right?

Let's compare the audiences for these two reports:

Report to the research team. After thinking about your research team members, you may conclude that what you need to do is inform each of them about the status of other team members' experiments, the precise findings to date, and the next step to be taken. You may also need to talk about the budget—how much has been used and how much remains. You'll probably want to include precise details of your findings and progress on the new product, the next experiments and tests to be completed, what you want to determine, and a time schedule for each team.

Report to the board of directors. Picture each board member and assess what he knows about the organization's R & D program. Maybe there are board members who have no background in your industry and know nothing about the R & D process. What they may be most interested in knowing is how much money has been spent and how close you are to having a competitive product ready for market. They may also want to know what the profit potential is. Use this information to write the kind of report that will be on target and can be easily understood. It may even be instrumental in getting funding approval for the next R & D phase.

The answers to *who* your audience is and *what* he knows about the subject will help you begin to organize your message into the details you need to communicate: *what, why, where, when, who,* and *how much . . .*

To guide you, make notes about your audience. You may have to do some research on your audience members in order to properly aim your report.

Remember, the audience dictates both your approach and the content of your report.

WRITING PURPOSE

Just like you need to know *who* your audience is, you must know *why* you are writing. You must have a clear *purpose.* This step is often missing from the business writer's initial thinking process, and the result is an email that is very fuzzy and unfocused, or that has no perceivable purpose, and thus adds no value.

To avoid this, ask yourself: *What do I want the audience to do after reading my report? Is my purpose to* inform *my reader,* entertain *him (unlikely),* persuade *or* convince *him to accept my point of view,* motivate *or* inspire *him, or* instruct *him?* Determining this will help you properly form your message.

MESSAGE STATEMENT

Begin to build your message on the framework of the audience you've identified and the purpose of your communication. Think through what you want to communicate until you can concisely state your complete message in a single sentence—a message statement. The simpler and shorter, the better. While distilling what you want to say is hard work, it's well worth the effort. It will save you lots of time in the end. See chapter 3 for more help.

Think through your message objectives until you can write a single sentence that distills:

- ▶ Who your reader is
- ▶ Why you need to write

> ▸ What you need to communicate
> ▸ The action you want the reader(s) to take after reading your communication

Here are a couple of examples of message statements for what will become fairly complex R & D reports. The first report will be written to *inform* the research team about new deadlines; the second report will be written to *motivate* the board of directors to approve more R & D funds.

Message statement for report to research team: We need to correct errors, curb costs, and meet the deadlines of September 15 and October 30 in phase 3 to stay on schedule.

Message statement for report to board of directors: Our new product line can make $7.2 million in new profits each year with $2 million in additional funding.

The message statement doesn't give the details of the *what, when, why, who, where,* or *how much,* but it makes you, the writer, do the hard work of thinking through your message from beginning to end and of focusing your thoughts. This will result in speeding up your writing process and delivering a much better communication—one that is focused, organized, clear, understandable, and well documented and supported.

ORGANIZE

Once you have your message statement firmly in mind, or even while you're thinking through what you want to write and forming your message statement, start the next step of further organizing your thoughts. Make a few notes under the major points of your message; begin to scratch out a rough outline (the next steps of outlining are covered in detail in chapter 2). Here are a couple of examples from our R & D report.

NOTES FOR RESEARCH TEAM REPORT

> ▸ Experiments status: 67 percent complete
> ▸ Findings: tolerances too high

- ► Next step: reduce tolerances and error rates
- ► Budget remaining: 33 percent
- ► Scheduling: deadlines for test completion, September 15 and October 30

NOTES FOR BOARD OF DIRECTORS REPORT

- ► New product development status
- ► Profit potential the first year: $7.2 million
- ► Ready for market projections
- ► Budget spent: 67 percent
- ► Additional funding needed: $2 million

YOUR WRITING VOICE

"Be yourself when you write," William Zinsser admonishes at the end of his chapter on business writing. To make your writing easy to understand and approachable, write the way you talk—in a conversational tone.

When you're done, use this simple test to check your writing: read aloud what you've written. Hearing it is valuable. Does it sound conversational, like you'd speak to your colleagues if you were talking face-to-face?

If not, rewrite it. Remove the language that sounds stuffy or distances you from your reader. Now read it again, *aloud*. Much improved? Can you hear the difference?

CLEAR, SIMPLE, AND ACTIVE WORDS

Use clear and simple words and an active voice—where the subject acts—to make your message easily understood. There's always the temptation to flaunt bigger, fancier, and plumper words that send readers scurrying for their dictionaries. Resist it. And resist the tendency to fill your message with jargon, unless it's needed because it's germane to your subject and audience. Use concise and clear words that can't be misunderstood. This will draw your reader into your message, and it will engage him.

Once your message statements are complete and the points of what you will include in your message written down in a rough outline, flesh out your outline.

Next, write your lead or topic sentence for your first paragraph. The important thing to remember here is that you are making a deal with your reader with your topic sentence. You're telling him: "This is my contract with you: I'm going to 'pay off' on what I promise in this topic sentence and deliver the complete thought with what follows in the paragraph."

Topic Sentence for the First Paragraph of the Research Team Report

Don't start with this kind of passive, inert, and bloated construction: Implementation of the feasibility criteria was begun on April 15 with utilization testing calibrated to optimize operational performance objectives and to determine profitability of a prototype on a projected developmental budget of $3 million.

Instead, use an active voice with simple, clear words—like people talk: With a budget of $3 million, we began testing the prototype on April 15 to see how it would perform in a real laboratory.

Compare the two statements. Which one is clearer and gives you real information you can relate to? Try reading them aloud. How do they sound?

Now, how would you write that first sentence in a report to the board of directors?

Topic Sentence for the First Paragraph of the Board of Directors Report

Eliminate passive, foggy sentences that are stuffed with flabby nouns and vague adjectives: The allocated investment for the feasibility phase of implementation testing that commenced on April 15 has been reduced by two-thirds as of this date, with an additional infusion of another $2 million anticipated to be required in order to determine whether utilization of the present design will realize the profitability factor originally targeted.

If you were a member of the board of directors, you might respond, "What?" Oh, sure, you'd get it after rereading and pondering the sentence. But would you want to do that? Would you want to take the time? Did you get the point that the R & D team is requesting another $2 million? Or is the following statement, which uses a strong, active voice with understandable, simple words, clearer?

> Since April 15, we've spent two-thirds of our $3 million R & D budget developing an analyzer prototype, and we'll need another $2 million to deliver a profitable product.

WRITE, WRITE, WRITE

Let yourself go and write. Take your idea by the horns and release yourself to the task of writing from beginning to end, using the outline you created. This will usually produce the best and most comprehensive draft. It will allow you to *write in the flow*.

EDIT, EDIT, EDIT

It's easy to become very attached to what you've written and feel like you don't want to eliminate a single word. William Strunk, in *The Elements of Style,* is almost rabid on the point: "Omit needless words." This is true, times two, in today's blizzard of business communications. The reality is that most business writing benefits from ruthless editing. The best way to attack this is to let what you've written sit for a while to give it, and yourself, breathing time, objectivity. Walking away, even briefly, allows you to become more dispassionate about what you wrote, much more objective, and it lets you become constructively critical. You'll see it with fresh and clearer eyes, and thus be able to identify where you can eliminate a superfluous word, or several; substitute a stilted word with a simple, clear one; and eliminate those extra words that fog your meaning. You may even need to eliminate complete paragraphs or reorganize the entire document. (See chapter 2 for more help on this.)

Use the reading-aloud technique again here to test how your message sounds. If you can, have someone else whose opinion you respect read it to see if the message is crystal clear.

Yes, this process takes a little bit of time and some extra effort, but the payoff is a clear message that says very good things about your future as a business writer.

The following chapters will further unpack these steps to help you hone each skill that goes into making a successful business writer.

2

Create a Road Map

Now, with your message statement clearly written, you can start creating a more detailed plan.

ORGANIZE YOUR THOUGHTS

Once you've established the *need for your communication, know who your audience is,* and *have established what of value you have to say,* you're ready to begin the next step.

Ask yourself: *What do I want the reader to do after reading my communication?* This does three things: (1) it makes you focus on the purpose of your communication; (2) it helps you start to think about the logical order or structure your communication needs to take; and (3) it helps you decide if your writing will need to inform, argue, explain, advise, instruct, describe, persuade, inspire, or motivate. Or some combination of these. Think back to the department progress report. It will *inform* employees within your department about R & D progress and the deadlines. But our report to the board of directors will both *inform* and (hopefully) *persuade* the members to approve further funding.

Now ask yourself: *What is my reader's attitude about what I need to communicate?* Will your reader resist what you'll write? Will he be receptive? Eager? Hostile? This will further inform you about the approach and tone your writing needs to take.

Again, recount *what your reader already knows about this subject.* This will help you start your communication at the right place.

Looking over your notes, write down the main points you want to make and put them in logical order. For the short and simple communication, you're now ready to start writing. But be sure you narrow your focus to keep your communication on target. Here are a couple of examples:

TOO BROAD	PROPERLY FOCUSED
How can we institute better departmental reporting?	Will the weekly Form A produce more accurate departmental reporting?
How can we reduce carbon emissions?	Which catalytic afterburner, model D or E, will reduce carbon emissions better?

If you are writing a progress report, you'll undoubtedly just chronologically state what progress, if any, has been made since your last report. For a conference report, you will record the things discussed, decisions made, and expenditures authorized. You may also state future actions required and the people responsible for them, as well as the due dates. Minutes of a board meeting will cover the same items.

The long report or communication needs some road signs to be organized for easy reader understanding. Most readers of business communications will find that the skeletal order should be the following:

1. *Purpose / Objective / Executive Summary / Summary*
   This will offer the reader a synopsis of what you will present.
2. *Discussion/Findings*
   This will detail the facts.
3. *Conclusions*
   This will tell the reader how you arrived at your deductions or opinions.
4. *Recommendations*
   This may include the next steps to take, costs, projections, timing, or additional problems to be solved.

OUTLINE FOR DIRECTION

For a longer and more complex communication, like a business plan, a progress report, an annual report, a competitive analysis, a fundraising letter, or a white paper, you'll need to do more legwork (and brain work) before you begin your first draft. You'll want to build a good road map—an outline that will get you to your desired destination without time-consuming wandering in the wilderness of misdirection and side issues, or subpoints.

You may start by making random notes to yourself in an unorganized "mind mapping" or stream-of-consciousness order on a sheet of paper, then connecting the ideas with lines to show relationships.

Mind Mapping (Stream-of-Consciousness) Outline

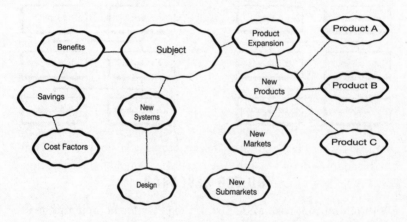

Now the most logical way to begin to think about your complex communication structure may be ordering the points according to (1) chronology (what happened first, second, third), (2) sequence (steps of a procedure), (3) spatiality (where something happened), (4) comparison (e.g., pros and cons), (5) analysis (unpacking the why of something), (6) division and classification, (7) deduction (general to specific), (8) induction (specific to general), (9) cause and effect, (10) increasing order of importance, or (11) decreasing order of importance. The type of communication, the audience, and your purpose will determine which will work the best.

For most complex communications, the easiest way to outline is to use Roman numerals or an alphanumeric outline. While such an outline may seem old-school, it will create the best road map and save you time and misdirection. And it will help you order your thoughts. Here's an example of an outline for a comparative report I used in my book *How to Write It*.

Alphanumeric Outline

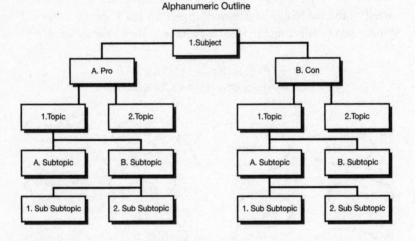

DO THE RESEARCH

With our current rush to be first, it's too easy to short-circuit the essential step of research. Don't. To prove your case or support your position, you'll need to start with a series of narrowly focused questions your audience wants you to answer. Do the hard work of thinking here. Develop these carefully. And, depending on the subject and scope of the communication, do a complete job of researching. You don't want to be blindsided by a study or vital facts that you overlooked and didn't factor into your communication. At the same time, you must be selective. Use only the best facts that will help your reader understand. And don't forget that your research may include your personal survey, inspection, or observations, if these are important.

Be sure of your facts, and state them in what Zinsser has described as a "linear sequence." That requires you to do the heavy lifting of thorough research and the hard thinking that places your progressive statements in their proper order. As Zinsser adds in his chapter "Science and Technology," "This is no place for fanciful leaps or implied truths. Fact and deduction are the ruling family."

And be sure to use facts objectively and honestly. Don't color them, inflate them to make your case, or distort them to shoehorn them into appearing to validate your preconceived argument.

Get out there and get into the research. Test-drive your ideas by seeing what is actually happening in the sales district in question, on sales calls that aren't producing sales, or in the distribution center where waste is too high.

Make a detailed record, and be meticulous in immediately recording the facts. You won't remember all the details, so you might even want to use some video backup to either remind yourself of the facts or incorporate in your communication. Like any reporter, you are looking to answer *what, why, where, when,* and *how much.*

FINDING SOURCES

Research has never been easier—or more difficult. What do I mean? There are countless research tools available to you without your ever having to leave your computer, but just because you find something online doesn't mean you don't have to test its validity. Use the old journalistic rule of locating three authoritative sources that agree, whenever possible. Use the best databases available for your subject area; read the best and most recent books; check government sources, when applicable; and even review and search things like blogs, when the subject requires it.

Evaluate your sources. Do they provide background information, define terms or concepts, supply evidence for your argument (or against it), and add support or lend authority to your argument or position? Now go back and see if you've answered your focused questions. And remember that your report must cover the complete picture—pros and cons.

3

What's Your Point?...
and Other Principles

Because everyone in business has too much to read, you need to make what you write inviting and concise. You can accomplish this by making your message clear, short, active, precise, and natural (conversational). But how?

MAKE IT CLEAR

Clear writing is achieved by clear thinking. And again I'll reemphasize: *think through what you're going to write until you can state it in a single message statement.* That's one sentence. So, take a little more time, practice, and work at it until it becomes almost automatic. It's well worth the effort. And it will pay off in time saved and effort greatly reduced.

Even writers of epic-length novels and lengthy screenplays are required to think through their creations until they can state their stories in a "high-concept" sentence—or not more than several. The movie *Alien* is reported to have been pitched to the movie studio in three words: "*Jaws* in space."

The international ad agency M&C Saatchi has the right philosophy for business writing: "Brutal Simplicity of Thought." Simple ideas enter the brain easier and stay there longer. And these simple ideas are produced by clear thinking. Yet we see the evidence of what William Strunk called "muddy thinking" every day in the emails we receive, the ads we read, and the other business communications that clog our email inboxes, or are expounded in business meetings.

MAKE IT SHORT

"If I'd have had more time, I'd have written a shorter letter" has been attributed to many writers, including Mark Twain, Cicero, Voltaire, Blaise Pascal, and Ernest Hemingway. It's a fact all successful writers come to know: *Shorter is almost always clearer. Better. More effective.*

Think back to some of the most confusing emails you've received. They were probably much longer than necessary. And dollars to doughnuts, they were dashed off before the writer thought through his message and before he applied the principle of hard thinking. That single act of haste undoubtedly resulted in the rambling, disorganized, and fractured or half-baked email that arrived in your inbox. Or the email that was followed by one, two, or more additional emails from the same person, wherein he tried to clear up what he'd said in the first. Instead of receiving clear, effective communication, you ended up frustrated and confused.

A recent email appeared in my inbox from a board member of a journalists' organization who was responding to a request for input on a proposed new policy. The message read, in part, "Just to clarify my earlier email . . . I must really put all my facts together, and think through what I want to write before I start. . . ." This from a journalist with over twenty-five years' experience. And true. This was the fourth long, fractured, and confusing email on the topic from this member, and it meant that a dozen other board members had spent a substantial amount of time trying to knit together what the writer wanted to convey. And it still wasn't clear. It resulted in a dozen emails posing questions to the original poster. In the end, the writer confessed (in yet another email) that she had not done an essential step of communicating—gathering her facts before she began writing.

Once you have identified and come to know your audience and assessed what he knows about the subject, have done any required research, and have thought through what you have of value to add (if you can't add value, don't write), then distill your message into a short and simple message sentence, like one of these:

We can save $2 million a year on production line C by making three simple changes.

We can increase productivity by 23 percent by using the new incentive plan.

Let's create a new lunch rule that eliminates the 12:30 p.m. chaos in the cafeteria.

Or make it even shorter: We should stagger the lunchtimes.

Now you've done the hard thinking that will get you out of the blocks without faltering, and you've put yourself on the straight path to clear and concise writing.

The second rule of short writing: *put the subject and the action verb up front to get your meaning moving.* It's called creating a right-branching sentence: the subject and verb of the main clause appear at the left, or the beginning of the sentence; the other elements branch to the right, or appear afterward. Here's an example of a right-branching sentence, written by Lydia Polgreen in *The New York Times* (italics are mine) and quoted by Roy Peter Clark in his book *Writing Tools*:

> *Rebels seized control* of Cap Haitien, Haiti's second-largest city, on Sunday, meeting little resistance as hundreds of residents cheered, burned the police station, plundered food from port warehouses and looted the airport, which was quickly closed. Police officers and armed supporters of President Jean-Bertrand Aristide fled.

Clark says, "Think of that main clause as the locomotive that pulls all the cars that follow." Then he adds, "Master writers can craft page after page of sentences written in this structure."

This offers the reader both clarity and energy. And it keeps him reading.

Everyone in business has too much to read—certainly too many emails. And nothing turns readers off faster than a ninety-five-page proposal that debates whether the new office furniture should be beige or seafoam. Just one look at a torturous and long introduction to a bloated and ponderous forty-word sentence—"In the interest of utilization, optimal visual appearance, and the prospect for the longest office wearability—" will have readers hitting the DELETE button. Deadly. A simple "we should buy the beige furniture" is really all we need.

Roy Peter Clark, in his book *How to Write Short,* even takes on the revered William Strunk's original credo: "Vigorous writing is concise. A sentence should contain no unnecessary words, for the same reason that a drawing should have no unnecessary lines and a machine no unnecessary parts. This requires not that the writer make all his sentences short, or that he avoid all detail and treat his subjects only in outline, but that he make every word tell." Clark's lean and clean (edited) version is: "Vigorous writing is concise. A sentence should contain no extra words for the same reason that a drawing should have no extra lines. Not all sentences need be short and without detail. But every word must tell."

Note how Clark has left the first (topic) sentence, which is short, as written. But he has replaced "unnecessary" with "extra," and he has trimmed the analogy while keeping the focus on writing. Doesn't the edited version say the same thing? Isn't it stronger? Certainly it's easier and faster to read. The word count has gone from sixty to thirty-seven—a savings of nearly half. And there was no loss of meaning.

When E. B. White became editor and contributor to *The Elements of Style,* he restated Strunk's classroom cry "Omit needless words" with "Write short."

Developing the habit of clear thinking, then short writing, is a great *time-saver.* It saves the labor of cutting what you've written by editing later, though editing is always a necessary step. William Zinsser said it well:

> Clear thinking becomes clear writing; one can't exist without the other. It's impossible for a muddy thinker to write good English. He may get away with it for a paragraph or two, but soon the reader will be lost, and there's no sin so grave, for the reader will not easily be lured back.

MAKE IT ACTIVE

Verbs are the words that express an action or state. The verb family is divided into three branches: *active, passive,* and *linking* verbs. Active verbs are used where the subject is acting; passive verbs, where the subject is being acted upon. Linking verbs express a state of being. They are most often a form of *to be* (*am, is, are, was, were, be, being, been*), and these *to be* verbs aren't usually active or passive.

> **Active verb:** The board *amended* the bylaws.
> **Passive verb:** The bylaws *were amended* by the board.
> **Linking verb:** Bylaw amendments *were made* by the board.

Passive verbs are often coupled with *to be* or its various incarnations: *be, am, is, are, was, were, being, been.* These are usually limp because they don't contain action. Compare these sentences:

> **Linking verb:** A power outage *was* the cause of the pump failure.
> **Passive verb:** The pumps *were fried* by the power outage.
> **Active verb:** A power outage *fried* the pumps.

Make your writing active by using active verbs. Active verbs are more vigorous than their passive cousins. They engage the reader, and they help carry your message directly to where you want it to go.

Yes, write in the active voice is good advice—but not always. There are times when you want to emphasize the receiver of the action or minimize the subject or actor. When the object of the sentence (or action) is more important than the subject, you will want to use the passive voice. In these cases, your best choice may be a passive verb:

- In step 3, the carburetor *is placed* in the engine.
- The shocks *must be attached* to the body at this point.
- Pencils *are being replaced* by pens in boardrooms.
- Time cards *are due* from department heads tomorrow.
- Expense reports *must be approved* by managers.
- A press release *will be issued* by the director of PR.

And sometimes the subject isn't the point (or isn't important) or just isn't that interesting. That's when you should use the passive voice:

- All replacement parts *will be ordered* by maintenance.
- New personnel policies *will be issued* on Friday by HR.

Scientific and technical writers often use the passive voice to emphasize the process or procedure rather than the actor. But the business writer should almost always put the subject to work by using active verbs. Which message from your bank is more satisfying to you, the customer?

- Your bank account *will be* managed by me.
- *I will* manage your account.

Wouldn't you rather hear the active voice from the person who is taking responsibility?

There are times, too, when you will want to use the linking verb *to be* to connect a subject to a noun that renames it or to connect the subject to an adjective or phrase that makes it more vivid.

Linking verb: Headquarters *is* the home of the Wilkins museum.

But when the *to be* verb makes the sentence weaker or longer or saps the energy or action, replace it. Note the difference in these statements:

- Leaving your post during work hours *would be* in violation of company production rules.
- Leaving your post during work hours *violates* company production rules.
- *Do* not *leave* your post during work hours.

In the third example replacing a noun with an imperative action verb both strengthens the sentence and trims the word count. (The subject is "you" understood.)

Don't drape your verbs with prepositional phrases or weigh them down with adverbs that suck the power out of them and muddle the meaning. And don't put them to sleep by turning them into "nominals," or nouns, by adding *-ing, -tion, -ment, -ance, -al, -y,* or *-ure.*

Using nominalizations: There is a *requirement* that all students have an *evaluation* of their transcripts for placement purposes or to meet a prerequisite.

Changing nominalizations back into verbs: The college *requires* that
the admissions office *evaluate* all student transcripts for placement and
prerequisites.

Check out these verbs and their nominal forms:

ACTION VERB	NOMINAL
direct	direction
construct	construction
provide	provision
inflate	inflation
submit	submission
attend	attendance
fail	failure
master	mastery
deliver	delivery
appraise	appraisal
refer	referral
assess	assessment
advance	advancement
evaluate	evaluation
perform	performance

And then there's the verb that becomes a noun, called a *gerund,*
after you add *-ing.* Here are some examples:

ACTION VERB	GERUND
work	working
advise	advising
estimate	estimating
provide	providing
submit	submitting
attend	attending
direct	directing

- *Rowing* is a great sport.
- *Gathering* data can become a distraction.
- *Moving* is recommended as a solution to clutter accumulation.

A quick caution: Yes, active voice is usually the gold standard, but don't overdo the power-verb approach by putting it in every sentence, or it becomes repetitive, monotonous, and produces a hyped (imperative) tone that can turn readers off. Don't risk losing the appeal that a variety of sentence structures offers.

MAKE IT PRECISE

The most maddening email that turns up in inboxes is the one stuffed with general and opaque words and long sentences with run-on construction. It may brim with phrases within phrases and jargon that is not known by the reader. These emails mask rather than expose the writer's message—if, in fact, he has one. They say nothing. The writer has managed to waste the reader's time. Completely. This kind of noncommunication has been aptly named "gobbledygook," "legalese," "technobabble," or "bureaucratese."

The reader will give it a sentence or several. He may even stick it out for a paragraph or two if it's from the boss. But it's misery. And in frustration, he'll reach over and hit DELETE.

The lack of precise writing can also signal that the writer doesn't have anything of value to add, but wants to be counted as "weighing in"; hasn't thought through what he wants to say, starts writing instead of thinking, and must mask his words in an effort to disguise his lack of a clear message; or is so mired in muddy thinking that he can't distinguish his ass from first base (to borrow an expression).

Don't let that writer be you.

It's the writer's job to create meaning for the reader. Your writing becomes oatmeal if you don't use precise, specific, and strong descriptive words to carry your message. Select the exact word that best expresses your meaning. Or don't write.

Bill Walsh, in *Lapsing Into a Comma,* says it well at the beginning of chapter 4, "Literally Speaking: Write What You Mean, Mean What You Write," when he points out that reporters sometimes don't report specific details of the news, for example, to avoid doing the research necessary to learn what those details are. The same is true, times two, of the business writer.

Not only does the business writer need to research until he gets the details right; he needs to think in specific terms that are meaningful to his audience.

A word about jargon. When NPR asked listeners what jargon terms were specific to their business, Hawaiian whale watchers offered up the term "flying pickles," which sounds mystifying and absurd to most of us, but in communicating with other Hawaiian whale-watching guides, it's the best and shortest way to say they see baby humpback whales breaching near their boat, and other guides would do well to get their passengers alongside to enjoy this rare and fascinating sight. If the guide adds that the flying pickles are "mugging," it's even more exciting, because it means the baby humpbacks are coming close to the boat and breaching to take a look at its passengers.

So, it's important to clear up this jargon confusion. When jargon words are understood by your audience, make your message easier for your readers to understand, make your message shorter or more concise, and make your message more conversational, use them.

Use precise nouns and vivid verbs to create clear mental pictures for your reader. Make sure that dynamic verbs and strong nouns are the heart of your style. Which terms below create the clearest picture?

GENERAL OR VAGUE	PRECISE
students	English 101 freshmen
women	young females between eighteen and twenty-four years old
hammer	tack hammer
screwdriver	standard Phillips-head screwdriver
cough medicine	Sudafed maximum strength
valve	red-capped valve A (see diagram)

Here are some comparisons you may recognize:

GENERAL OR VAGUE	PRECISE
Exceeded the budget	Overspent by $50,000
Delays have resulted	Five weeks behind schedule
Expenditures exceeded projections	$45,000 over budget was spent

While the precise terms may be longer than their general counterparts, this eliminates confusion and promotes understanding for the reader.

Even more than nouns and adjectives, vivid verbs create strong impressions, and they do more than almost anything else to improve prose. Consider these contrasts:

ANEMIC VERBS	STRONGER, PRECISE VERBS
advance	go
go back	return
leave behind	abandon
light up	ignite
put into action	act
will be cleaned	clean
is repaired	repair
to help	help
will be prepared	prepare
is going to be	will

Precise writing also requires that you drop redundant modifiers and delete unnecessary phrases. When President Franklin D. Roosevelt read this sentence: "We are endeavoring to construct a more inclusive society," he revised it to read, "We're going to make a country in which no one is left out."

Here are some examples from the list "Use Simple, Direct Words," in my book *How to Write It*:

INSTEAD OF	USE
analyses were made	analyzed
activate	begin
add the point that	add
10 a.m. in the morning	10 a.m.
achieve purification	purify
absolutely essential	essential
accounted for by the	caused by
actual experience	experience

adequate enough	adequate
along the lines of	like
am in receipt of	received (or "have")
as of this date	today
despite the fact that	although
during the year of 2015	during 2015
in the interest of time	[eliminate]
in the majority of cases	most (or "usually")
give an indication of	indicate
have at hand	have
in order of importance	order
in the event of	if
in the neighborhood of	about
in the normal course of our procedure	normally
in view of the fact that	because
is found to be	is
is indicative of	indicates
is suggestive of	suggests
it appears that an oversight has been made	I [or "we"] overlooked
it has been brought to my attention	I have learned
it has been recognized that	[eliminate]
it would not be unreasonable to assume	assume
the fact that	[eliminate]
the purpose of this memo	[eliminate]
there is no doubt	[eliminate]
what is believed is	[eliminate]
with reference to	[eliminate]

Untangling obtuse writing to make it friendly and readable is worth the effort.

MAKE IT NATURAL (CONVERSATIONAL)

Chatter on Facebook, Twitter, and the ever-growing crop of other Web sites commonly appears in slang, conversational shorthand, and new and increasingly outrageous acronyms. It's strange, then, that when it comes to business, writers too often lapse into a centuries-old, starched-and-stiff form of the King's English. You'd never recognize the report that shows up in your inbox as coming from the guy in the next office with whom you cheer for the local sports team and share the occasional joke in the coffee room. He has one "talking voice" and another "business writing voice." Why is that?

Adding a formal flair to your business writing isn't the way to go. What you write is easier to understand if you write it in simple, conversational English. Give yourself this test: Record yourself in general conversation, maybe one of those sports debates from your end of a telephone conversation; then listen back. (Record your end of the conversation only.) Then read aloud that report or proposal you just finished and compare the two. Sound the same? No? My point, exactly.

Now, attack what you've written in that stilted form. You might start by speaking a simple synopsis of your message. Or go back to that message statement you wrote before starting. Rewrite it the way you'd say it in conversation.

As a check on yourself, reread aloud what you've written each time. Do you hear where you are missing the mark? Read the following statements aloud and listen for the difference:

Stuffy: Departmental employee progress reports are due and must be delivered to the human resources (HR) office by 5:00 p.m. each Friday from this point forward. Requests for exceptions to this rule will not be entertained, nor will such requests be granted under any circumstances.

Conversational: Turn in employee progress reports to HR each Friday by 5:00 p.m. No exceptions.

Even complex ideas—especially complex ideas—benefit from a careful effort to condense and to eliminate unnecessary words. By streamlining your writing, you help your readers understand—and that is the point, after all.

TIPS

- Don't use novelty words in a quest to be unique or clever; your objective is to write a clear message.

- Avoid jargon that can cloud your message; but if technical words are the most precise and best for your audience, use them.

- Cut to make your message clear; but reducing the word count is only the beginning of your job.

- Replace the verb "to be" with an active verb in most of your business writing.

- Use precise details to make your message clear.

- Change nominals (noun forms) to verbs to energize your writing.

- Use precise nouns, and avoid using layers of descriptive adjectives to make your meaning clear.

- Make sure your sentence construction is clear and straightforward.

4

Write, Write, Write

A recent neuroscience study, reported on by Carl Zimmer in *The New York Times*, looked at novice and accomplished fiction writers to determine how the creative brain works. The study, conducted by Dr. Martin Lotze and his colleagues at the University of Griefswald in Germany, compared the fMRI scans of both groups of writers, first during brainstorming and then during writing. When novice writers were brainstorming, their scans showed more activity in the visual centers of their brains. By contrast, the brains of expert writers were more active in regions involved with speech.

Dr. Lotze conjectured that the two groups were using different strategies. He thought the novices were watching their stories like a film in their heads, while the experienced writers were narrating their writing by using their inner voices.

During the writing phase of the study, another distinct difference emerged. Inside the experts' brains, the region called the caudate nucleus, the part of the brain that plays an essential role in developing and using a skill that is honed by practice, including activities like playing board games, became very active. In the novices, the caudate nucleus was quiet.

In the first stages of learning any kind of skill, we use a lot of conscious effort. Then, as the skill develops with practice, our actions become more automatic. The study shows that in the creative brains of the expert writers, the caudate nucleus was more active because the practice of writing had become much more automatic.

Conduct your own study. Read some of your competitors' prose, and see how you can make yours simpler and smarter. If you have done the hard work of thinking through your message, you'll find the writing phase much easier. And the skill of writing well for business will become more automatic with practice.

If you've listed the main points and subpoints of what you want to write, you'll find your message flows more easily out of your brain and onto the computer screen.

To demonstrate this flow principle to creative writing students, instructors often use an exercise that has been named "hot writing." Here's how it works. Participants are instructed to write for a period of time, maybe five minutes or ten minutes or even twenty minutes, without taking a break. Their writing, they are instructed, is to begin after they are given a setup statement to finish. The statement might be to tell a story that begins with a hypothesis like "This is how I felt when he said . . ." Or they may just be instructed to freely write about how they are presently feeling physically or psychologically. The instructions are usually as follows: (1) let your mind (or imagination) go; (2) write for the full time without stopping; (3) don't reread or edit yourself; (4) don't lift your pen from the paper or ponder your next thought. Just write.

You, the business writer, can take a cue here. If you have written your message statement, made notes about what you want to write, and have done any preliminary research to line up the facts, you're ready to just start writing. Below, I explain how I strongly suggest you proceed.

1. GIVE YOURSELF THE ASSIGNMENT

A recent session at the Aspen Ideas Festival assembled creative leaders from a cross section of disciplines to talk about how and when they were most creative. The common thread that ran through all disciplines was that creativity happened when these people were constrained by a project with a deadline and the pressure to produce an excellent product. It was, participants reported, a disciplined exercise of needing to produce—and produce on time. Waiting for the muse was not an option.

2. BRAINSTORM

Remember, clear thinking produces clear writing. You might want to bounce your ideas off a colleague if the writing assignment is something like an important proposal or a dynamic report. In fact, a brainstorming session, or several, before you start can help expose and eradicate any remaining murky thinking on the topic.

3. SET ASIDE TIME TO WRITE

And make sure it's free from distractions. When you have a writing assignment—self-imposed or handed to you by the boss—block out time without distractions. Schedule uninterrupted time to work. Denounce the lie that you can multitask. This is the time to employ the principle of creativity and write uninterrupted without stopping.

Chances are, you won't be tempted to stray off course after you get started, because you will be energized first by your sense of purpose and then by accomplishment.

4. EXPECT TO WRITE WELL

Feeling confident is very important. Build your confidence by reviewing your message statement again to reaffirm your objective. Think. Put any additional thoughts into your outline under the proper heads and subheads. This can bolster your expectation of writing well.

My own writing process for this book began by realizing the need for better business writing. I interviewed many business managers, who experience daily the need for better business writers. I thoroughly examined in-depth scientific studies, surveys, and experiments that have been done on this topic. With this information in hand, I developed the following message statement: "Writing well is necessary for success in business."

I made a lot of notes along the way and kept files of many facts, study results, surveys, and experiments. Slowly, the points of my basic outline—which later became the chapters in the table of contents of my book proposal—developed, and I kept adding subpoints and notes under each.

When I started the actual writing of this book, I felt confident that I had the bull by the horns. Would it be a breeze? Not even close. But

I knew where I was going with the writing, and I knew I had a very good road map to get me there. I was confident. (Now you will be the judge of whether that confidence was well placed!)

5. WRITE FROM BEGINNING TO END

Doing so will help you get down your complete message in the best and most efficient way, and will allow you to write in what creative writers often call the "flow." The document won't be your polished and final one. It will be your first "rough" draft. But this essential step is the most important.

If you get *really* stuck, go back a few sentences and reread what you've written to get yourself back on track, and keep the continuity of thought and voice. But don't do it often. And resist the urge to start rewriting at this point. What you want to do in this step is to get the whole thing down.

6. USE YOUR NOTES

Successful business writers use their road map—the outline—to stay on course. Keep it where you can see it; and trust your notes to take you in the right direction and get you to your destination. You spent time and effort in building your outline; don't abandon it and go off-track. Trust it and write straight for the first-draft finish line.

7. KEEP IT REAL SIMPLE

As I mentioned in the last chapter, stuffing your writing with complex, run-on sentences, bloated and tangled phrases, and dangling strings of modifiers doesn't fool anyone. This kind of writing only signals that it is the product of muddy thinking or evidence of a lazy or ignorant writer.

This doesn't mean you should "dumb down" your writing. Patricia O'Conner, in *Woe Is I*, warns us not to confuse simplicity with simple-mindedness. Your aim is to add value—real value—whether it's an entirely new idea in the form of a proposal or a routine production or travel report. And adding value is best accomplished by writing in clear, simple words. This means eliminating those pompous and empty phrases and baggage that add nothing, or even detract from your meaning. Here are some examples you would do well to deep-six:

in the matter of	I am in receipt of your
after much study of the matter	in the interest of time
reached a consensus of opinion that	deemed it necessary to
on the basis of	in regard to
with regard to	the purpose of this email
until such time as	the fact that
in the majority of instances	what is believed is
there appears to be	there is no doubt
in the opinion of this writer	may I call your attention to
it must be said	it is the intention of this writer to
as a statement of fact	it is noteworthy that
as to the future of	it has been recognized that
until such time as	perhaps I should mention that
I am writing in response to your	

8. USE THE ACTIVE VOICE

Make the subject do the acting, and place an active verb next to it. You won't always use this straightforward construction, but it's a great general rule. Here are some examples of clear, simple writing and some examples of the muddy variety.

Don't write: There has been an allocation of $40,000 as a line item in the budget, which was designated to remediate deterioration of the physical facilities, which are in need of extensive renovations to improve optimal function.

Write: We budgeted $40,000 for repairs.

Don't write: After a contracted discussion, an allocation of an additional $1.25 per hour in remuneration for production employees was approved through an affirmative vote by the board of directors.

Write: The board of directors voted to give production workers a $1.25 per hour raise.

Don't write: After extensive and exhaustive testing, a substantial elevation of 25 percent in the amount of calories expended was determined.

Write: Test results show a 25 percent increase in fat burning.

Don't write: Through comparative analyses of the production records from last month and this month, there appears to be evidence that the net increase in net production for this month exceeded last month's figures by approximately 33 percent.

Write: Production is up 33 percent this month.

Don't write: As far as the orientation meeting is concerned, it has been decided that all new employees are required to be in attendance.

Write: New employees must attend the orientation meeting.

Front-loading a sentence with the subject and verb gives it energy and eliminates the possibility that the reader will become confused or lost. While using a prepositional phrase to start the sentence allows you to give the reader information about the subject and allows you to vary the sentence structure (which can add interest), using a simple construction should be your first choice. Still, here are some examples where starting with a prepositional phrase makes good writing sense:

- *When assembly is complete*, plug in the power cord.
- *Before the meeting*, please make sure the boardroom is prepared.
- *To apply*, contact the human resources department.
- *In an emergency*, leave your workstation immediately.
- *Between paragraphs 1 and 2*, please insert chart A.

In these sentences, the beginning phrase actually shortens the sentences by quickly orienting the action of the subject, which is "you" understood. As you can see, this construction works very well for sentences that instruct the reader. It's great for instruction manuals and things like employee policies and procedures.

When you separate the subject and verb by a lot of words, you risk confusing, or even losing, your readers. Here's an example:

- A *change* in the standard operating procedure, which is the fact that purchase orders must be approved before ordering, *is being considered* by the CEO, and he will render his decision next week.

This contorted construction may cause the reader to have to give the sentence a second go before he can understand. Because you want to emphasize *change* in this sentence, you'll want to lead with that. But you can clear things up, energize the sentence, and make it easier on the reader by rewriting:

- The CEO may *change* the standard operating procedure for approving purchase orders. He *will announce* his decision next week.

The first sentence has thirty-three words; the rewritten two sentences have nineteen words. Is the first or the second clearer?

Writing a sentence to delay introducing the subject and the verb works well for the creative writer of fiction, who is trying to build tension. But this is not the job of the business writer. The business writer needs to demystify his message and make it crystal clear. In his chapter on business writing, William Zinsser states his four writing "articles of faith: clarity, simplicity, brevity and humanity," which brings us to the next important rule of business writing.

9. WRITE SHORT SENTENCES

Writing short is the most direct route between the beginning and the end. It helps you reach your goal of writing so that your audience will understand, and it helps convince your audience to react the way you would like them to. Roy Peter Clark, in *Writing Tools,* says of short writing forms: "Their brevity gives short works a focused power. . . ." This certainly applies to business sentences. Count the words in five of your sentences. How many are there? If you have sentences of over thirty words, you need to cut them down to size.

Of course, you'll want to vary your sentence length to add interest and avoid monotony—you don't want your message to read like a telegram or a tweet—but try to write short.

10. USE EXACT, SPECIFIC, STRONG WORDS AND THE RIGHT TONE

There are anemic, vague words, and there are exact, strong, precise words—usually words with verbal muscle. Don't risk losing your reader by using weak and opaque language, which casts your message in doubt. Opaque language is the trick of those who are uncertain or don't have anything of value to say. Compare these phrases:

TOO GENERAL	SPECIFIC
the meeting	the June 21, 2014, production meeting
all affected employees	production line A employees
your employee rules set out the requirements	item number 10 in your employee manual states
on Tuesday morning	at 10:00 a.m., Tuesday, July 10, 2014

Using exact words leaves no room for confusion and increases the power of your writing.

Check out the difference between these two lists of words:

ANEMIC	WORDS WITH VERBAL MUSCLE
secure	get
proceed	go
procure	get
initiate	start
indicate	show
transact	do
visualize	see

Beware, too, of using hedging or "weasel" words, such as "generally," "possibly," "perhaps," and "it could be," that broadcast your unwillingness to commit yourself or your lack of anything of substance to say.

Let's compare the writing of three authors. This first passage is the opening paragraph of the prelude to *Middlemarch*, by George Eliot, written in 1866. It is considered by many experts to be the best novel ever written:

Who that cares much to know the history of man, and how the mysterious mixture behaves under the varying experiments of Time, has not dwelt, at least briefly, on the life of Saint Theresa, has not smiled with some gentleness at the thought of a little girl walking forth one morning hand-in-hand with her still smaller brother, to go and seek martyrdom in the country of the Moors? Out they toddled from rugged Avila, wide-eyed and helpless-looking as two fawns, but with human hearts, already beating to a national idea; until domestic reality met them in the shape of uncles, and turned them back from their great resolve. That child-pilgrimage was a fit beginning. Theresa's passionate, ideal nature demanded an epic life: what were many-volumed romances of chivalry and the social conquests of a brilliant girl to her? Her flame quickly burned up that light fuel; and, fed from within, soared after some illimitable satisfaction, some object which would never justify weariness, which would reconcile self-despair with the rapturous consciousness of life beyond self. She found her epos in the reform of a religious order.

Now, read the opening paragraph from the prologue to Katherine Boo's book *Behind the Beautiful Forevers*, published in 2012:

Midnight was closing in, the one-legged woman was grievously burned, and the Mumbai police were coming for Abdul and his father. In a slum hut by the international airport, Abdul's parents came to a decision with an uncharacteristic economy of words. The father, a sick man, would wait inside the trash-strewn, tin-roofed shack where the family of eleven resided. He'd go quietly when arrested. Abdul, the household earner, was the one who had to flee.

The Eliot excerpt is beautiful and veiled in meaning. It was written to make the reader ponder its meaning and savor the language. The Boo example is exact and transparent, causing the reader to get, immediately, a very clear and precise picture.

Here's a third example from the prologue to Elizabeth Warren's book *A Fighting Chance,* published in 2014:

> I'm Elizabeth Warren. I'm a wife, a mother, and a grandmother. For nearly all my life, I would have said I'm a teacher, but I guess I really can't say that anymore. Now I'd have to introduce myself as a United States senator, though I will still feel a small jolt of surprise whenever I say that.

Don't you feel like this is how Elizabeth Warren would speak to you if you were in a conversation with her? You, the business writer, want to aim for the kind of transparent and clear style of the last example.

11. KEEP RELATED WORDS TOGETHER

You make your job, and your reader's job, much easier if you keep verbs close to the subject and modifiers close to the words they modify. The result is less rewriting for you and a clear message that your reader can easily understand. Look back at the subjects and verbs in Katherine Boo's opening paragraph:

> midnight was
> woman was
> police were
> parents came
> father . . . would
> he'd go (he would go)
> Abdul . . . was

Notice that the descriptive modifiers, parenthetical phrases, are placed immediately after the subjects:

> father, a sick man,
> Abdul, the household earner,

This is clear and powerful writing at its best.

Look back at Elizabeth Warren's paragraph, and note the location of the subject and verb:

I'm
I would have
I . . . can't
I'd have
I will

You don't have to struggle to get the meaning here. It doesn't take a second or third reading. It's crystal clear.

12. WRITE LIKE YOU TALK

You might go back to the advice in chapter 1: record your end of a telephone conversation or listen to how friends talk during off-hours about sports and politics. Take note of the number of multisyllable words they use. How does this compare with the number you used in that announcement about Friday's meeting? How about last month's production report or that quarterly sales report? Make what you write conversational, and you'll keep your readers interested.

A bit more about jargon: You often hear a caution to avoid jargon in business writing, and this is both true and false. And let's be sure to define jargon here as those special words unique to a particular industry. When you're writing to a general audience, or an audience unfamiliar with the inside language or special terms essential to your business, it is excellent advice to avoid jargon that your audience may not understand. But when you are writing to insiders, professionals in your field, jargon is often the best choice because it is the most direct language to carry your message. A zillion years ago, when I was a technical writer producing user manuals and industry technical reports, it would have been silly for me to try to find substitute, simple words of a syllable or two to replace ones like "chromatography," "spectrometry," "molecules," "integrator," "autoanalyzer," and "capillary." My audience,

inside technical and engineering people, knew exactly what these
words mean, and they would have been confused if I'd have used sub-
stitutes.

But even while using these words, I had to make the writing conversational, precise, and easy to understand. My caution was to avoid
lapsing into a formal and obscure language to go along with these four-
and five-syllable words. That's your caution, too.

Beware of "buzzwords." There is another caution here that I should
mention: avoid the "inhuman," stilted sludge that now gums up business conversation, and sometimes writing across industries—what *The
Wall Street Journal* has labeled "buzzwords." The newspaper's editors
recently asked readers to contribute the ones that set their teeth on edge.
Many are invented and contrived words that began life as sports expressions. Others crawled off social media Web sites and into the lexicons
of business-speak and business writing. What's your reaction to these?
Are any turning up too frequently in your inbox? In your writing?

tee up	skate where the puck is going to be
change agent	wheelhouse
proactive	strategic mindshare
intuitive	viral
robust	it is what it is
strategically	paradigm killer
epic	monetize
move the needle	turnkey
runway (as in "running out of runway")	incentivize
	24-7
thought leaders	gamify
quantify	bandwidth
skill set	onboard
game-changing	sustainable
at the end of the day	open the kimono
score a touchdown (or "score")	bleeding edge
take it into the end zone	push the envelope
hit it out of the park	delayering
native advertising	dynamic resilience
iconic	out-of-the-box thinking

big data   hard-wired
going forward   touch base
low-hanging fruit   bottom line

13. START EACH PARAGRAPH WITH
A TOPIC SENTENCE

Just as your message statement focuses your thoughts for your complete message, a topic sentence at the beginning of each paragraph focuses what you'll tell the reader. It's your promise to the reader that this
is what you'll deliver in the paragraph. What follows, then, must pay off
on that promise, but it will be a promise much easier to keep because
in thinking through the content of your paragraph, you will have organized your thoughts.

Here are several examples:

- Our test results showed improvement.
- Sales volume in the last quarter showed a substantial increase.
- The new policy will be put in place.

Now the reader knows what you'll deliver in the paragraph.

14. KEEP PARAGRAPHS SHORT

What happens when you look at a report with paragraphs that cover
most or all of your computer screen? Maybe you'll give it a quick glance,
then decide to print it out to read later because you're sure it will be
time consuming to read and digest. Or you might flip it into something
you call your reading file. The point is that long paragraphs are a turnoff
to the reader. Break paragraphs up into their logical parts.

Short paragraphs signal to the reader that this won't consume
huge amounts of time to read. He can read, understand, and respond
quickly. Again, you'll want to vary the length in a long document for
added interest, but in business writing it's important to keep your paragraphs short.

15. USE HEADS AND SUBHEADS

When writing a report of more than a few paragraphs or a business proposal, use the points and subpoints of your outline to create heads and subheads. This not only breaks up your communication but also gives the reader a guide for finding details he wants. Underlining and using boldface type will add both visual interest and reader direction. But don't overuse these.

16. SUMMARIZE

Certainly a single-paragraph announcement about an upcoming conference doesn't need a summary; a twenty-five-page progress report on a construction project does. An important point to be made here is that the summary may not be a conclusion, and it may not draw a conclusion. It should briefly summarize the points of your communication. If there is a conclusion, it should briefly state it. This is where clear thinking and short writing are especially important.

For many types of proposals and detailed reports, you will need an executive summary, which is labeled as such and placed at the beginning of your communication. It should be short, concise, and cover what you will state in detail in the document. The operative word here is "short." The executive summary serves as a synopsis of what you're going to say or an abstract of what will be presented. In the case of a proposal, it may also set down the terms of the RFP (request for proposal) that is the basis for your communication.

When I pitched a prospective client for a new public relations program, I started with this executive summary:

> ● At the invitation of Mr. Rollo, MC Corporation is submitting this
> proposal describing how we will increase public awareness of
> the XYZ Corporation by 25 percent through use of a combination
> of (1) press releases, (2) social media blogs and tweets, and
> (3) a series of editorial opinion pieces.

5

Revise, Revise, Revise

With your first draft written, breathe a sigh of relief. It was hard work, and you did it. You got the entire message down! Don't dive right back in to reread what you've written. Take a break, and congratulate yourself. You have created a piece of whole cloth from which to work. You've completed your first draft.

When you're ready and can take a fresh view, then it's time to reread your draft. Zinsser tells us that "most first drafts can be cut by 50 percent without losing any information or losing the author's voice." So your job is far from finished. And if the document you've drafted is long, complex, or very important, you may need to go through a few more drafts.

The next step, revising and rewriting, will require a sharp and clean cutting tool and an objective attitude. This is the machete phase, or the large scissors phase. It's where you will make the big cuts.

Even Zinsser admits to rewriting and revising chapters of *On Writing Well* four or five times. Yes, four or five! He writes, "With each rewrite I try to make what I have written tighter, stronger and more precise, eliminating every element that is not doing useful work."

The need to revise and rewrite goes double for the business plan, the quarterly or annual report, the corporate history, or the client proposal. Plus, of course, you'll bring in a number of other people after you've finished making the big revising cuts and before you begin the final polishing—editing—stage of completing an important document.

Before you reread your document, focus on three things:

1. *Think about your audience.* Get into his mind-set. Is your message aimed for his understanding?

2. *Review your message statement.* Have you delivered what you set out to?

3. *Go over your outline.* Have you included all the points and subpoints that are needed?

Your rough (first) draft may be disappointing. But remember: you wrote it to create a whole from which you could carefully fashion a fine document. And that is exactly what you will do in the rewriting and revising stage.

Consider this list as you begin to reread your draft. Did you accomplish these goals?

Use the reader's point of view. Have you written it for your reader's understanding, considering what he knows about the subject? Will it be clear to the reader what you are trying to accomplish? Will your document inform or persuade your reader? Will he react in the way you intended?

Reorganize. Read it again for logic and order. Is the progression of thought and proof of fact complete? Reorder and rearrange words, sentences, paragraphs, and even sections to make things clearer.

Add information. Have you included all the facts needed to prove your case?

Eliminate. Don't spare the delete function, or the red pencil, if you have printed out a copy and are revising it. Remember Zinsser's words: most documents can be improved if reduced by half. Yes, half.

Check your facts. The carpenter's rule of measuring twice and cutting once is a good one. Double-check all the facts you have included. Nothing will undermine your case like inaccuracy.

Be sure the tone is right. Near the top of the list of executive complaints about unskilled business writers is the fact that they are tone-deaf. They don't get it right. What they write is strident, offensive, or simply not in tune with their readers. The current trend toward snarkiness on social media has undoubtedly crept into business writing. It's important that your message is pitch-perfect. Read your draft aloud and imagine how you would interpret it if a colleague sent it to you.

Sometimes revising means starting over and rewriting from the beginning. Don't despair. This is a technique used by many creative writers. They expect the first draft to be their first attempt of at least several.

Your organization's protocols may require a number of reviews and approvals after your second draft stage. When I worked for the Joint Commission, it was my job to write the standards used for inspecting health care facilities to determine the quality of care they were delivering. My council was made up of a diverse group of doctors, nurses, and administrators from across the country, who reviewed a copy of each draft of the standards I wrote. The process of incorporating their suggestions and changes, and reconciling their different opinions often took a dozen revisions.

When I worked as a technical writer of maintenance manuals, specification sheets, and equipment sales brochures for a medical instrument company, I had a very different set of reviewers. Every piece I wrote had to be vetted by engineers, technicians, marketing people, and users in the field. Sometimes as many as fifteen drafts were written before all the reviewers approved a final draft that was then ready for the editing process.

Writing the second draft, or the third or fourth, if necessary, will be easier because your thinking will be much clearer. But be sure to take a break between each draft to regain some objectivity. And don't circulate review copies to your colleagues until you are sure you have completed the revision and rewriting steps to your satisfaction.

If you are in doubt, have a colleague—preferably one you trust and one who is an expert in the field, but not part of your review team—read through the draft. You may want to ask for his general impressions; you may want him to critique your draft; or you may want to ask him questions, such as, Do you understand the purpose of the document? Is the tone right for an audience of regional salesmen? Does this inspire you to increase sales in your district? Have I answered every question you might have about the sales bonus?

When your draft is well organized and you feel all the other elements are included, it's time to start the next step of small cuts—editing.

6

Edit, Edit, Edit

It is time to fine-tune what you've written. Polish to make perfect. If you are working on a short business communication, you'll do this step after completing your first draft. Or your second. But if you are doing a long or complicated document or a crucial piece of advertising copy or a marketing report, you will start editing after you have finished making the large cuts of revising and rewriting described in chapter 5. You may have produced five or six drafts by now. You may also begin the editing after your final draft has circulated to a colleague or two, to a review group who must approve it, or to a reviewer you've asked to take a test read.

Give it fresh air. The first step in editing is to *take a breather*—take some time from what you've written—at least an hour or two, or overnight, whenever possible. This is particularly true if you've produced quite a number of drafts, have obtained the approvals required by your organization, and are ready to do the final polishing. It's amazing how much more objective you can be and how you can begin to view your "brilliant" prose in a fresher and more critical light.

Kill your darlings. Let's face it, we all sometimes fall in love with what we've written, even in the business world. But after your prose has had just a bit of time to age, you will be able to distance yourself and cut your draft down to its clearest and most concise best. You'll be able to eliminate those beautiful sentences that are really just fluff or opaque gobbledygook. You'll see those needless phrases, extra modifiers, paragraphs that add nothing, and sentences that just aren't essential to the message. Elmore Leonard said, "I try to leave out the parts that people skip." Here's where you take the last precise cut to eliminate everything that isn't essential.

Print it. Sometimes printing out what you've written before you read it allows you to see it more clearly. For important communications, try this and see if it works for you.

Check tone. In the first chapter of my book *How to Write It,* I make the point that "writing is really talking on paper, so make your communication talk."

Read aloud. There's no better way to check for a conversational tone than reading what you've written aloud. Hearing it is key to catching stiff phrases; overloaded, run-on sentences; and repetitions.

Don't repeat. When you are talking, you may repeat yourself for emphasis, particularly if you are making a speech. When you write, don't. Read through what you've written and look for sentences or phrases that repeat. Strike the weakest one(s), and leave the strongest. (The duplicates will pop out if you read your work aloud.)

Example: In step 4 you will be installing the cartridge into the cartridge holder. Locate the cartridge holder inside the machine (see figure 5), and insert the cartridge into it.

Nothing wrong with that, is there? It's clear, fairly concise. Could you shorten it? Make it even more concise? Clearer? Let's eliminate the first sentence since the second sentence gives the reader the information he needs.

Correction: 4. Locate the cartridge holder inside the machine (see figure 5), and insert the cartridge into it.

By using the 4 in front of "Locate," you don't need the first sentence.

Cut needless words and phrases. Editing requires precise cutting of unnecessary modifiers, confusing or repetitious phrases, or words that just aren't working hard enough. This is the stage when you streamline your communication to its shortest, clearest, and most concise.

Take another look at the example sentence:

4. Locate the cartridge holder inside the machine (see figure 5), and insert the cartridge into it.

I think you can do even better. What else can you cut? Do you need the entire first part of the sentence? The "see" within the parenthesis? The end of the sentence? Cut this sentence down to its essential best:

Final: 4. Insert the cartridge into the holder (figure 5).

Since you have an illustration, you can cut the original sentence of twenty-six words down to six. Was any meaning lost? No. Does it use the active voice? Yes. Is all the deadwood of extra words eliminated? Yes.

William Strunk, in *The Elements of Style*, said, "Although there is no substitute for merit in writing, clarity comes closest to being one."

There is often a reason for obscurity in writing fiction—you may want to build suspense, create mystery, or mask your exact meaning so you can reveal it later. But there is no excuse for obscurity in business writing. Here clarity wins the day—and the promotion for the business writer.

Strunk advises, "When you become hopelessly mired in a sentence, it is best to start fresh; do not try to fight your way through against the terrible odds of syntax. Usually what is wrong is that the construction has become too involved at some point; the sentence needs to be broken apart and replaced by two or more shorter sentences." Mark Twain backs that up: "I notice that you use plain, simple language, short words, and brief sentences. That is the way to write English—it is the modern way and the best way. Stick to it; don't let fluff and flowers and verbosity creep in." Well said. He must have been thinking about business writing.

Write simple, clear sentences. Look for those contorted sentences that you can't easily untangle. Examine them for their essential idea(s). When the sentence contains more than one complete thought, break it into two. Or three. Here's an example:

- Our extensive analytical testing procedures of the economic influences affecting trends within our industry have resulted in

the drawing of some very important conclusions about the
essential need to restructure our marketing department in order
to maintain the uppermost competitive position in comparison
to our competition.

Besides removing the words in the sentence that make it bloated and
vague, what else do you think would help this sentence? Does it need
a complete rewrite? Yes. How about this?

- In order for us to remain number one, our economic-trends test
  shows we must restructure our marketing department.

We have reduced the sentence from forty-six words to nineteen. It's
shorter. Is it clearer? Yes. Does it have more impact? Yes. We're on our
way!
　Or, how about this?

- To remain number one in marketing, here's what our economic-
  trends test found.

Or,

- Here's how we can remain number one in marketing, our trends
  test shows.

These last two sentences reduce the word count even further. Can
you rewrite it even shorter?

Eliminate obscurity. This means eliminating evasive, opaque language. Read this:

Example: XYZ Company is proud to announce the new addition of an un-
rivaled, large-scale, complex capability process and technology that will
propel our cutting-edge organization into a whole new mode of operational
sophistication as yet unseen in the marketplace.

What? The sentence has forty words that manage to say nothing.
What, exactly, is new? Foggy, complex words are often used to hide the

fact that the writer has nothing to say. Or that he fears being the employee who commits himself to a course of action. Or fears being the person who is the first to state what everyone suspects is fact. Maybe there is something new and important that could be stated clearly if the writer is willing to say it. Certainly the use of some real, hard facts and numbers would turn the sentence from opaque (and ineffective) to vigorous (and clear).

Correction: We will launch the X software on Friday. This product will increase our sales by 32 percent by identifying new customers.

We have reduced the forty words in one sentence to nineteen words, one letter, and one number. And we've actually said something.

What do you make of this statement?

Example: Complex Wireless Systems seamlessly integrates a vast array of complex consulting and outsourcing capabilities across the full life cycle of business operations within an international marketplace to optimize every transformative possibility . . .

What does the company do?

Correction: Complex Wireless Systems is a one-stop source for helping organizations change.

We've reduced the word count from thirty-one to twelve. This example would also benefit from facts and figures.

Here's one more:

Example: Our new promotional consumer perception campaign will be developed, implemented, and executed to allow us to determine, within fairly accurate tolerances, what consumer opinions are when presented with the new model X.

Correction: We will learn what consumers think of model X with this campaign.

Or, if we want to emphasize the campaign, we would invert the sentence:

- With this campaign, we will learn what consumers think of model X.

Editing here made the sentence short—with much more impact— and clear.

THE FINAL EDIT

After you have defogged your message, it's time to do the final edit— to make those small and precise cuts—in order to correct any typos, grammar blemishes, or construction errors. You'll probably do this after colleagues in your department or group or someone else you've asked has read it and offered suggestions, and after you've incorporated any changes they suggest that improve the document.

Make a checklist. Go through your document once for each point of correction. Some writers find this the best way to make sure their documents are perfect. Your list will probably include these questions:

- ▶ Is the purpose of my message clear?
- ▶ Have I kept the focus on my audience? Have I addressed them properly?
- ▶ Is the information I've given complete? Have I answered the *what, why, where, when, who,* and *how much*?
- ▶ Have I presented information in a logical order?
- ▶ Does the prose flow?
- ▶ Is my message compelling and easy to read and understand?

If the answer to these questions is yes, then it's time to do one final check, paying attention to the following sticky details.

Beware the -ly words. Check for the use of those pesky adverbs that were inserted to add strength or definition to verbs. Usually, they drain power from the verb. Strunk says, "Words that are not used orally are seldom the ones to put on paper" and "Do not dress words up by adding *ly* to them, as though putting a hat on a horse."

Adverbs that may drain power from, or confuse, verbs:

overly
thusly
decidedly
conclusively
remotely
considerably
purposefully
admittedly
usefully
systematically
organizationally
needlessly
substantially

Look at each sentence and see if you can make it stronger by omitting *-ly* words.

Example: He was *overly* cautious about the use of *purposefully* aimed sales incentives.

Correction: He was cautious in his use of sales incentives.

Have we lost shades of meaning in the rewrite? No. If you want to state that "he" was too cautious, use facts instead of inference.

Omit words and phrases that repeat. The following repetitive words and prepositional phrases should be struck from your writing. Use one word or the other, but not both. Once you tune in, you'll find others.

WORDS THAT REPEAT

past history
still remain
continue on

past experience

future plans

tall skyscraper

new discovery

sultry humidity

various differences

each individual

basic fundamentals

true facts

cash money

test experiment

important essentials

future plans

same identical

end result

final outcome

sum total

past history

sudden crisis

free gift

PREPOSITIONAL PHRASES THAT REPEAT

in the case of

in the article

in this example

for the sake of discussion

in a manner of speaking

by way of example

in the meantime

for your reference

in the event of

Delete useless phrases. In an attempt to be conversational, you may sometimes add useless phrases that just slow the reader down. They don't make your writing more conversational. Eliminate them.

PHRASES THAT ARE USELESS

in a sense

I will add (I might add)

it is interesting to note here

it should be pointed out

to say it more simply

due to the fact that

with the possible exception of

until such time as

in the interest of time (or "in the interest of being brief" or "in brief")

at such time as

in consideration of these facts

for the purpose of

if I do say so myself

if I might add (may add)

if you will

that said

unless or until

at this point in time

as a consequence of

at this juncture

before we begin

I can assure you that

in light of the fact that

in a sense

it could be said that

consideration was given to

this document is in response to

Remove qualifiers that weaken your writing. By including qualifiers, you brand yourself as a hedger, a person who suffers from the fear of commitment, or someone who pads your writing by using wiggle (waffle) words that sap the strength from your sentences or kill the message altogether. Adverbs like "partly," "mostly," "completely," and "extremely" can also be qualifiers. Remove them.

Have you answered the *what, why, when, who, where,* and *how much*? Use real facts and figures.

QUALIFIERS THAT WEAKEN YOUR WRITING

almost

sometimes

only

very

quite

might

just

enough

maybe

really

a little

less

pretty

try

perhaps

with luck

perchance

consider

hope to

I believe

in my opinion

I suppose

I suggest

I think

probably

almost

still

very well might be

may be, or maybe

sort of

a bit

seems like
a portion of
certainly
extremely
completely
exactly
entirely

Use verbs for more power in your writing. It's easy to fall into the habit of writing in the more abstract: using nouns (including gerunds). Replace them with verbs to strengthen your writing.

DON'T USE	USE
consideration	consider
judgment	judge
observation	observe
conclusion	conclude
direction	direct
failure	fail
provision	provide
inflation	inflate
assessment	assess
attendance	attend

Clear away any jargon and buzzwords. You'll annoy readers by lacing your writing with hackneyed, vapid words and phrases. These vary by industry and change frequently. Using them infrequently can be effective, but peppering your writing with them labels you as someone who either has nothing to say or is afraid to say something. According to recent manager surveys, here are the top offenders:

absolutely	address the issue
accountability	aggregate (used as a verb)
achieve clarity	agile
action items	all-hands
actualize	alternative analysis paralysis

aperture moments

architect

at the end of the day

audacious

ballpark

been there, done that

benchmark(ing)

best of breed

best practices

big data

big picture

blamestorming

bleeding edge

blue-sky thinking

bottom line

brainstorm(ing)

brain surgery

branding

bucketize

buy-in

cash neutral challenge

champion (used as a verb)

change agent (or catalyst)

change management

chart it out

circle back

circle the wagons

client focus(ed)

client-wiring

closure cluster

collaborate

color

coming to fruition

communications channels
    (synonym for "media outlets")

compelling

conceptualize

content

contribution

core competencies

corporate values

cost-effective end-to-end solutions

credibility

cross-platform

cultivate our resources

culture

customer-centric

customer-focused

cutting edge

deep dive

deliverables

delta

disintermediate

diversity

dog and pony show

doing more with less

double down

downsize

downward trend

drill down

drinking the Kool-Aid

drinking water from a fire hydrant

dysfunctional

ecosystem

emotional leakage

employee engagement

empower

emulate

enable(r)

end to end

engaged

enterprise-wide

envisioneer

e-tize

excellence

experiencing slippage

exponential

face time

facilitate

fact of the matter

fast track

first mover

flattening

flexible

flounder

flowchart (used as a verb)

framework

front-end functionalities

full-service

full-service solutions provider

full solution

fusion

future proof

game changer

gap analysis

get on the bus

get our ducks in a row

glass is half-full

globalize

goal-oriented

goal-setting

going forward

go the extra mile

guesstimate

guiding principles

guru

half-pregnant

hard stop

have a dialogue

heads-up

headwind

health break

herding cats

high-level view

holistic approach

hypos

ideation

impactful

implement

in-market for ("in the market for")

incentivize

info

infomediaries

initiative

innovate

inspect

integrated

intellectual capital

in the front of the bus

in the loop

involuntary retirement issue

it is what it is

key

key player

knowledge base

knowledge management

leading

leading edge

leading provider

let's not boil the ocean

let's sharpen our pencils

level-setting

leverage

literally

living document

logistics

long-term

lots of moving parts

low-hanging fruit

low risk, high yield

make hay

make the ask

matrix (used as a verb)

mentor(ing)

methodology

mind-set

mindshare

mission-critical

mission statement

monetize

morale

move the needle

moving forward

multitask(ing)

nailing Jell-O to a tree

napkin (used as a verb)

negative growth

net-net

net present value (used as a verb)

network(ing)

new synergy

nimble

north of

not rocket science

on a (time frame) basis

110 percent

on the same page

on us

on your/my plate

open the kimono

operationalize

optimalization

optimization

out of the box

out of the loop

ownership

oxymoron(ic)

peel the onion

percolate

performance-based

performance management

personal branding

ping

position (used as a verb)

power shift

price point

principle-centered

prioritize

priority (used as an adjective)

proactive

process review

productize

profitable growth

proprietary

provider of value-added services

pushback

push the envelope

quality vector

quick and dirty

ramp up

reach out

reality check

recontextualize

reengineer(ing)

refresh

regroup

relative to

repurpose

resonate

resource constrained

result(s)-driven

revisit

rightsize

risk effect

risk management

robust

rock and a hard place

rocket science

rock star

ROI

rounding error

rubber-stamp (used as a verb)

run it up the flagpole

scalable

scenario

schedule compressed

sea change

seamless

service organization

singing from the same hymnal

skill set

smartsize

socialize ("communicate with" or "publicize through social media")

social media

social media crisis

solutioning

solutions-oriented

south of

squared away

stakeholder

stand-alone

state of the art

strategic fit

strategic gap

strategic synergy

strategy

streamline

(super)highway

sustainability

synergy, synergize, synergistic

tactical

tailwind

take it to the next level

take that off-line

talking points

task force

team (dynamics, player, building)

that said

the cloud

the writing's on the wall

thinking outside the box

30,000-foot level

360-degree survey

throw under the bus

tiger team

tighten the loop

timely ("on a timely basis")

tip of the iceberg

top of the house

total-quality ("driven" or "management")

touch base

touch points (media outlets)

traction

train wreck

transition (used as a verb)

transparent/transparency

trending toward

turf it out

turnkey

24-7 (or 24/7/365)

ubiquitous

unpack (when used to mean exploring the ramifications of something)

utilize

validate

value-added

value-driven

vertical	what you expect
vertical integration	whiteboard
vision statement	win-win
Web-enabled	within a reasonable time frame
Web 2.0	world-class

Don't forget to remove the generous peppering of those tired sports terms:

drive the lane	on the board
drop back and punt	play hardball
drop the ball	play team ball (be a team player)
fly ball	point man (guard)
full-court press	run point
game changer	score
game day	softball
game face	spitball (used as a verb)
game plan	suit up
get to first base	superstar
hit it out of the park	swim lane
home run	take it into the end zone
lob it	take it to the hoop
on base	tee up

Make sure subjects and verbs are close together and that modifiers are close to the words they modify. You'll be surprised how many problems of construction are solved by following this simple rule: *he decided; the red valve; they reached.* Don't leave doubt or make the reader reread.

Verb tenses need to agree. If you are writing in the past tense, be sure all your verbs match up in the sentence, paragraph, and section. If you use a summary or conclusion, you may change the tense to present or future.

Limit the use of pronouns, and make sure they agree. Don't lose the reader in who is doing what. It's better to repeat the subject for clarity than make the reader wonder.

Once more with feeling. If you're not sick to death of what you've written, you may need to go over it just once more. Give it another breath of air, come back fresh, and pretend you are the reader.

Have you, the writer, done what you set out to do? Will your reader respond in the way you desire? Is your information complete, concise, and stated with vigor? Yes? Then it's ready to go!

It's refreshing to read something like this online ad:

> Woot.com is an online store and community that focuses on selling cool stuff cheap. It started as an employee-store slash market-testing type of place for an electronics distributor, but it's taken on a life of its own. We anticipate profitability by 2043—by then we should be retired; someone smarter might take over and jack up the prices. Until then, we're still the lovable scamps we've always been.

It's conversational, concise, and reader-focused.

EDIT THIS

I was both the plaintiff and the defendant in a recent court action. Three cases were being rolled into one because they were interrelated. I and the opposing plaintiffs (two people), who were also defendants, were required to meet with a mediator to try to craft a settlement agreement before the case appeared before the judge. After considerable negotiations, we reached an agreement, and the mediator, a Harvard Law School graduate, used the court-settlement template to write the final agreement. She edited, reedited, then edited again, and finally produced this final document (blanks replace details here):

> . . . Plaintiffs agree to pay to the Defendant the amount of $_____ to resolve all issues between the Parties. Plaintiff has made a payment today in the form of cash for $_____. Plaintiff agrees to pay monthly payments of $_____ beginning on July 5, 2014 to the defendant's address listed above and the fifth of each month thereafter. There is a grace period of 5 days. If the Plaintiffs fails to make the monthly payments, the Court will issue a Judgment against the Plaintiffs for the balance due. Defendant agrees to

exercise a good faith effort to . . . This will resolve all issues between the parties with prejudice . . .

In court, the judge read the short agreement and looked puzzled. "Who is the plaintiff?" he asked the mediator. "Who is the defendant?"

After the mediator gave extensive explanations, the judge inserted the proper names after the first "Plaintiffs," and my name after the first "Defendant." He inserted an *s* after "Plaintiff" in the third sentence, which made the verb form wrong. The gavel came down, and the fractured document became the official record.

Take another look. What errors do you spot? Is "Plaintiffs" used consistently? What about subject and verb agreement? Is capitalization consistent? Could this have been much simpler and more concise? Try your hand at editing it.

Did you come up with something like this?

. . . Plaintiffs, Mr. A. and Ms. B., agree to pay to the Defendant, Ms. L., the amount of \$_____ to resolve all issues between the Parties. Plaintiffs have made a cash payment of \$_____ today. Plaintiffs agree to pay monthly payments of \$_____ on the fifth of each month (with a five-day grace period for receipt) beginning on July 5, 2014, to the Defendant at her address listed above, until the total of \$_____ is paid. If the Plaintiffs fail to make the monthly payments, the Court will issue a Judgment against them for the balance due. Defendant agrees to exercise a good faith effort to . . . This will resolve all issues between the parties with prejudice . . .

TIPS

- Nearly everyone's writing benefits from cutting.

- Remember, reading what you've written aloud will let you hear the sentences that aren't working and what doesn't sound conversational.

- Think often about your reader, what he knows about the subject, and what you need to tell him. Then think about what you want the reader to do after he reads your communication.

PART TWO

PERFECT WHAT YOU'VE WRITTEN

Write with Style, Voice, and Tone

We all have read the work of those writers of novels, personal essays, short stories, and even editorial opinion pieces whose style and voice we recognize after only a few sentences, or a paragraph or two—even before we see their bylines. But can the business writer be recognized the same way? No, not often. In business writing, concise, direct prose trumps personal style. But still, it's possible to sound like yourself and be recognized as the author of those great progress reports, that convincing and well-written business plan, and especially those memorable speeches and presentations.

Gaining the reputation as a top business writer when the results of what you write are measured by the ultimate standard of reader comprehension and persuasion wins the day—every time.

So strive for the things that connect you to your reader and let your style come after.

In fields like advertising, a distinct and clever voice and style will distinguish you from your competitors. But in most other fields, the ability to write clutter-free, clear English is king.

How, you may ask, if I've followed every step of chapters 1 through 6, do I create a message with style? Something that sounds like me? Something that is going to help me distinguish myself at work, and still connect me to my readers? You might argue that all you'll be left with are simplistic subjects and naked verbs. You may agree with Bill Walsh's words in *The Elephants of Style*: "I like a little writing with my writing."

I know I've harped on this point, but listening to your writing will help you write better. So will reading, reading, reading excellent business writers. And it will help you develop your own distinct style.

Here's a simple test: Read aloud a few of those writers you admire and mark the places that exhibit great rhythm, style, and tone. Then read something you've written that has a similar audience and purpose, and that requires about the same tone. How does your writing stack up? Have you varied the rhythm to make your writing interesting and pleasing to hear?

It may sound silly, but personal style actually begins with someone else. The more you read and ponder the style of others who write well, the more you will see how they develop and express their ideas. This will help you develop your own personal style.

Also read widely in other areas of business. And don't neglect the columnists who make their living doing this, like Thomas Friedman, George Will, and many others. Pick up magazines that so expertly distill business news, like *U.S. News & World Report*. And be sure to read magazines that cover topics in depth, like *The New Yorker, Architectural Digest*, and *The Atlantic*. An examination of these publications will help you understand great writing.

Read for meaning, and consider how the pieces were organized and constructed. Zinsser, in *On Writing Well*, states:

> There is no style store: style is organic to the person doing the writing, as much a part of him as his hair, or, if he is bald, his lack of it. Trying to add style is like adding a toupee. . . . This is the problem of writers who set out deliberately to garnish their prose. You lose whatever it is that makes you unique. The reader will notice if you are putting on airs. Readers want the person who is talking to them to sound genuine. Therefore a fundamental rule is: be yourself.

So, the trick here is to begin to think in clear patterns that will lead you to develop your own style and a strong voice.

Listen for voice, rhythm, and tone as you read. It will help you develop your own. Your voice must be your own, true voice, and still be appropriate to the subject matter (and occasion) and the reader. A tall order? Yes, but you can do it. Remember, what you aim for is to have a conversation with the reader.

The first hindrance to obtaining a unique style in business writing is the fact that the first person is often not used. This distances you, the writer, from the writing and from your reader.

Try this: Write something in the third person; then read it aloud. Sound cold? Clinical? Now write something in the first person and read it aloud. Which sounds more natural and contains something of yourself—your "voice"? This illustrates the problem of writing with style for business.

"Writing," Zinsser points out, "is an intimate transaction between two people, conducted on paper, and it will go well to the extent that it retains its humanity. Therefore I urge people to write in the first person: to use 'I' and 'me' and 'we' and 'us.'" Zinsser advises, "Even when 'I' isn't permitted, it's still possible to convey a sense of I-ness. . . . Good writers are visible just behind their words. If you aren't allowed to use 'I,' at least think 'I' while you write, or write the first draft in the first person and then take the 'I's out. It will warm up your impersonal style." This is very good advice for the practicing business writer.

Often business writers fear "going out on a limb," committing themselves. It is the second obstacle to writing with clarity and voice. It accounts for all those weasel-worded and waffling messages we receive. All we have to do for a living example is turn on the Sunday-morning talk shows where politicians are being interviewed. We have a front-row seat for the circus of long-winded answers that are filled with wishy-washy, weasel-worded, hedging nonstatements. Some call it the bob and weave.

Read a lot and identify styles you like. *Imitate.* Yes, imitate. "Never imitate consciously," warns Strunk, "but do not worry about being an imitator; take pains instead to admire what is good. Then when you write in a way that comes naturally, you will echo the halloos that bear repeating."

In developing your own style in business writing, you'll need to know your business culture forward and backward. Banking and finance aren't usually the home of breezy first-person reports. But if you are writing a letter to a customer, you will want to use the first-person reference if you want her to know you are her go-to person. Or if she wants a loan or a mortgage.

Remember, great communicators are made. They aren't born. So don't conform. Develop a personal style that's distinctive and straightforward.

Read the writing of excellent writers again and again to see how it works. Read for voice and style to find your own.

Tone is where you meet your reader—the point of connection. And remember, the tone of your writing needs to match both the occasion and the reader. When you understand your reader and the occasion, the appropriate tone will be easy.

Remember: if you need to write in a formal tone, that doesn't mean that what you write has to be stiff and petrified. It doesn't have to be inflated with four- and five-syllable words or contain a long parade of descriptive adjectives.

For interest, you'll want to vary the cadence, length of sentences, and maybe even change up the formal and informal. (Yes, you can occasionally insert an informal statement in a formal document.)

Style is—to be certain—a matter of personal taste. You can develop your own unique voice.

TIPS

- Read good writers in and out of your field, and listen for the voice, rhythm, and tone.

- Read good writers aloud to hear the rhythms of their sentences. Let them sink in.

- Take lots of notes and mark in the margins of magazines and books. Underscore points of construction, transition, and passages well stated.

- Read aloud from a draft you've just written. How does it compare to the masters?

- Continue this practice and see how you progress. If you want to hear it even more objectively, record yourself reading what you've written, and listen. In a couple of weeks or a month, do it again and see how you've progressed.

Punctuation Slam Dunks

You may be muttering that by the time we get to this stage of writing in the workplace, we should know where to put the period. Well, maybe and maybe not. It never hurts to have a quick review. Besides, there are those tricky bits, and the occasional odd placement that proves the rule by being the exception.

Here are a few simple rules to keep you out of the business writer's rough. Failing a basic point of punctuation isn't what you want on your résumé.

THE PERIOD

It should usually arrive much sooner than most business writers place it on their first draft. Run-on sentences, where periods appear only after several tangled thoughts, don't have enough of these little round players in the game. Those monstrosity sentences are a menace, and they can stop readers in their tracks.

Place the period at the end of each complete thought in a declarative or imperative sentence:

- Remove the cylinder.
- Report to the human resources department.
- The catalog lists several options.

Place a *period* after a compound sentence containing two independent clauses connected by a comma and a coordinating conjunction, by a semicolon, or by a semicolon and a conjunctive adverb:

- The reports are finished, and the meeting is scheduled for tomorrow at 10:00 a.m.
- Projections indicate an increase in sales, but a weak economy can thwart our estimates.
- Fire damaged production line A; therefore, those operations have been shifted to Plant B.

Place a *period* at the end of a complex sentence that contains one independent clause and at least one dependent clause. It subordinates one thought to another:

- After you complete your application, deliver it to the human resources department.

Place a *period* after a compound complex sentence that consists of two or more independent clauses and at least one dependent clause:

- For better accounting within your department, consult with Mr. Barnes in the CFO's office, and ask him to install the new software on your computer.

The period may also be placed after an incomplete sentence when writing in colloquial style and after sentences where the subject is understood. Use this approach sparingly to change the rhythm and cadence of your writing:

- Please respond by Friday at noon.
- They completed the report on time. At 4:00 this afternoon.

In the second sentence, the subject, "they," and the verb, "completed," are both understood.

Place the *period* inside parentheses and brackets when what appears within is a complete sentence, and outside when it is not:

- Employees must be trained in the new procedure. (Prior training in the old procedure doesn't count.)
- Insert the flange (after completing steps 1 and 2).

Periods are placed after personal titles and some abbreviations and in time designations:

Mr.

Mrs.

Dr.

i.e.

e.g.

ibid.

etc.

a.m. (or AM)

p.m. (or PM)

If one of these ends a sentence, don't use a second period:

● He arrived at 2:00 p.m.

No period is required after the U.S. Postal Service abbreviations for states, organization and country names, academic degrees, or era designations:

MI

CA

CO

UNESCO

FCC

NATO

USA

IRS

PhD

BS

BCE

BC

THE QUESTION MARK

Use a question mark after a direct question:

- Do you have the necessary supplies?

Don't use a question mark after an indirect question.

- He asked how we know when the assembly is complete.

THE EXCLAMATION POINT

Use the exclamation point after a sentence that expresses high feeling or deserves extra emphasis. Beware its overuse. It is very seldom needed in business writing.

THE SEMICOLON

Think of a semicolon as stronger than a comma and weaker than a period. It can take on either role, but it's usually used to signal a pause closer to that of a period.

A *semicolon* is very useful to link independent clauses or other sentence elements that are equal in weight and rank, especially when there are commas within the independent clauses. It helps keep things clear. This also applies when items in a series have internal commas. Use the semicolon between the items for clarity:

- Start by pushing the red, square igniter button; keep the igniter button depressed while pushing the green, oval accelerator button; and count slowly to four before releasing the two.
- The meeting was attended by Mr. Alex Rex, department manager; Ms. Ruth Baxter, personnel manager; and Mr. Ted Boxer, production supervisor.

Use a semicolon between independent clauses that aren't joined with a coordinating conjunction. (Independent clauses joined with a coordinating conjunction—*and, but, or, nor, for, so, yet*—are usually linked with a comma.) Here's how Charles Dickens demonstrated that use in the second paragraph of *A Tale of Two Cities*:

- There were a king with a large jaw and a queen with a plain face, on the throne of England; there were a king with a large jaw and a queen with a fair face, on the throne of France.

Here, too, Dickens has used the semicolon because each of his independent clauses contains a comma.

Use a semicolon if the relation between the independent clauses is clear (a semicolon may also be used with a conjunctive adverb like *however* or with a transitional phrase like *for example* or *in fact*):

- ▸ Production errors have been reduced; in fact, errors were down by 15 percent this month.
- ▸ Hold the wrench at a right angle; turn in a clockwise direction.
- ▸ Return all safety equipment to the proper place; for example, all fire extinguishers should be hung on their brackets.
- ▸ The board of directors will meet on Wednesday; all members should be prepared to vote on this issue.

SOME CONJUNCTIVE ADVERBS

accordingly	meanwhile
also	moreover
anyway	nevertheless
besides	next
certainly	nonetheless
consequently	now
conversely	otherwise
finally	similarly
furthermore	specifically
hence	still
however	subsequently
incidentally	then
indeed	therefore
instead	thus
likewise	

SOME TRANSITIONAL PHRASES

after all	in consequence
as a consequence	in fact
as a matter of fact	in order of importance
as a result	in other words
at any rate	in summary
at the same time	in the next step
even so	namely
for example	that is
for instance	therefore
in addition	thus
in conclusion	to the contrary

THE COLON

Use the colon to introduce a list or preceding something that illustrates or amplifies what has come before it:

- You have three choices: (1) file your application with HR; (2) request that your supervisor recommend you; or (3) call directly 000-000-0000.
- The study involves three groups of samples: rubber membranes, polycarbonates, and hot tar.

Use a colon after an independent clause to introduce a quotation:

- The rule is very clear: "Be at your station at 8:00 a.m."

Use a colon after an independent clause to call attention to an appositive:

- Mr. Reed has two counts against him: leaving his station and failing to clock out.

There are common uses for the colon that you won't usually have any trouble with. But let's list them. Use a colon in a formal letter after a salutation, between the hour and the minutes when indicating time, to indicate proportions, between a book or paper title and the subtitle, and in bibliographic listings between the city and the publisher:

- Dear Mr. Rankle:
- The classroom ratio of students to teachers is 15:1.
- *How to Write It: A Complete Guide to Everything You'll Ever Write*
  New York: Random House, 2013

PARENTHESES

Parentheses denote a "by the way" relation to the text. Use parentheses to signal that what's inside supplements the sentence. It's an aside, a minor digression, or even an afterthought. It's not as close to the sentence as the words after a dash or the words set off by commas.

- All entries for this week's competition are due by noon on Friday. (The results of last week's competition will be posted later today.)
- The new price structure will go into effect September 15, 2014. (All bids made with the current price structure will be honored through September 14, 2014.)
- Apply for the new benefit package by June 1, 2015. (If you have applied, your application is being processed.)

BRACKETS

Use brackets to enclose words, phrases, and sentences that you have inserted into quotations to denote that what is inside isn't part of the quotation:

- "This instrument [model A49] is not needed in the new procedure."
- "The HR [human resources] Department will handle this."
- "They [the production department] set a record."

Use brackets with the Latin word "sic" to indicate an error in the quote:

- "Don't exced [*sic*] your authority."

Use brackets sparingly. Overuse interrupts the flow of your prose.

THE HYPHEN

The hyphen is underused, and its absence often leaves us grasping for the real meaning of a sentence. Use it between compound modifiers to make your meaning clear:

- The dual-spray atomizer is designed for laboratory use.
- The small-business man may apply for this loan.
- The blue-code alarm requires an immediate response.

Use two or more hyphens between the words of adjectival phrases to make the meaning clear:

- Four three-prong-plug outlets are available in the office.
- The come-as-you-are invitation applies to all guests.

Use a hyphen between an adjective and a noun when it makes things clearer. Rules are a bit cloudy here because there are usually three choices: use two words; hyphenate; or combine the two words into one:

- container ship, container-ship, containership
- policy holder, policy-holder, policyholder
- work bench, work-bench, workbench
- gear box, gear-box, gearbox
- fly wheel, fly-wheel, flywheel
- motor mounts; motor-mounts; motormounts

Your choice will depend on your accepted industry culture.

It's perfectly acceptable to use the hyphen to shorten what you're writing when you want to show separated words are connected:

- Either the four- or five-step procedure will work.
- Order the three- or four-battery set for a reduced price.
- The one- or two-holiday policy may apply.

Use a hyphen to separate numbers, like Social Security numbers, telephone numbers, and ISBNs:

- 000-00-0000
- 1-800-555-5555
- ISBN: 978-1-60774-032-2

THE DASH

Use the dash to set off parenthetical material when you want to give it special emphasis. On your computer, use two hyphens (--) to create a dash (—). There should be no space before, between, or after:

- All production employees—including those who are part-time— must be instructed in the use of the safety equipment.
- All forms must be turned in by Friday—without exception.

The dash is a bit more dramatic and less formal than a colon, which is another choice in setting off a parenthetical phrase.

Don't fall into the habit of overusing the dash, or your writing will look like a telegram, and the result will be choppy writing that slows readers down or turns them off.

THE SLASH

The slash, or forward slant (/), has become ubiquitous for listing URLs. The backslash (\) is used for computer directory paths:

- https://united.com

The slash is used informally for all numeral dates: 4/11/14. (But don't use it on formal documents.) There's no space between the slash and the numbers that precede or follow.

Use the slash (forward slant) sparingly to indicate options or alternatives: he/she, his/her, and/or, either/or, hot/cold, World War II/Second World War:

- Each employee may elect his/her option from the list.
- Use the hot/cold valve to increase/decrease the temperature.

The slash is also used in paragraphs where you are quoting two or more lines of poetry, to show the line breaks:

- Emily Dickinson's words always inspire: "Hope is the thing with feathers / That perches in the soul, / And sings the tune without the words, / And never stops at all."

ELLIPSIS

Use the *ellipsis*, three spaced periods (. . .), to show where you have omitted material from a quotation:

- Page 5 reads, "You must submit full documentation . . . in order to qualify."

THE COMMA

The comma, so often overused or else forgotten, doesn't always have ironclad rules about usage. But remember that the comma's job is to make things clearer. It's that little road sign that makes things clear by telling the reader to pause.

Charles Dickens, in *A Tale of Two Cities*, demonstrated the comma's best use in his opening sentence (which was also the opening paragraph):

It was the best of times, it was the worst of times, it was the age of wisdom, it was the age of foolishness, it was the epoch of belief, it was the epoch of incredulity, it was the season of Light, it was the season of Darkness, it was the spring of hope, it was the winter of despair, we had everything before us, we had nothing before us, we were all going direct to Heaven, we were all going direct the other way—in short, the period was so far like the present period, that some of its noisiest authorities insisted on its being received, for good or for evil, in the superlative degree of comparison only.

Dickens used seventeen commas in that sentence. I'm not advising that you do the same. But Dickens demonstrates that the comma is a very useful tool for any writer, if used correctly.

Here are some guidelines.

Use the comma to separate independent clauses that are joined by one of the seven coordinating conjunctions: *and, but, or, nor, for, so,* and *yet*:

- Accounting will handle all orders, and production will receive job orders from accounting.
- He may elect to work regular hours, or he may choose the flex-time option.

Use the comma after an introductory clause for clarity and when the clause has a by-the-way quality:

- Of course, all options are on the table.
- In short, we will add three new features.

Use commas to set off parenthetical phrases:

- The meeting, if held in Richmond, will be well attended.
- The second option, my first choice, provides the coverage you want.

Use commas to set off nonrestrictive (but not restrictive) phrases:

- The spray, which has a shelf life of three weeks, works best for this application.
- The new policy, which is attached, goes into effect immediately.

The comma is used to separate coordinate adjectives that each modify the noun:

- A patient with an inflamed, tender-to-the-touch pancreas should not be put on this medication.
- Apply a clean, warm, dry compress.
- Perform each of the remaining preliminary, necessary steps in order.

But don't use commas if the adjectives don't each (separately) modify the noun. (If you can insert an *and* between the words, don't use commas.)

Serial commas may be used to separate words or numbers in a series to avoid confusion:

- You may choose red, green, or yellow.
- Options 1, 2, 3, and 4 are all possibilities.

Use commas to set off nouns of direct address, "yes" and "no," interjections, and interrogative tags:

- Please note, Mr. Wiggly, that the job is complete.
- The test was a huge success, wasn't it?
- Yes, the pump will be delivered today.
- Well, the decision must be final.

Commas should appear after "he said" or "she said" and before direct quotations:

- He said, "We will be finished tomorrow."

Use commas to set off the year from the rest of the date:

- On October 14, 2014, we moved to the new offices.

If the dates are inverted, as the Europeans do, commas aren't needed: 15 October 2014.

Insert commas after the parts of an address:

- Corporate offices are located at 211 South Industrial Avenue, Unit 101, Newark, New Jersey 11111.

Use commas to set off a title following a name:

- George Miller, MD, was appointed chief of staff.

TIPS

Don't be caught with your punctuation down. Here are some common mistakes you can avoid.

Don't Use a Comma

- Between dependent clauses—if they can't stand alone, don't insert a comma
- Between a verb and its subject
- To set off restrictive elements
- After a coordinating conjunction
- After *such as* or *like,* or before *than*
- If the subject of the action before an *and* or *but* continues to be the subject of the action after these conjunctions. (Use a comma if both sides of the sentence—before and after the conjunction—can stand alone.)
- In front of a parenthesis
- To set off indirect quotations (those that aren't direct quotes)
- After a question mark or an exclamation point in a quote in most instances

Don't Use a Colon

- After a dependent clause
- Between a verb and its object
- Between a preposition and its object
- After transitional phrases like *for example, such as, therefore, subsequently, including*

Don't Use a Semicolon

- Between independent clauses joined by a coordinating conjunction (*and, but, or, nor, for, so,* or *yet*)
- To introduce a list
- Between an independent clause and a subordinate clause
- Between an appositive and the word it refers to

9

Caution: Yield to Grammar and Usage—*or Not*!

Remember what I wrote in chapter 8: exceptions prove the rule? But when the exceptions keep piling up, it's time to take a hard look at the rule. Sometimes it's best to recognize that the rule just isn't working anymore (maybe never did), that the exceptions make sense and the rule doesn't, and that maybe it's high time to stamp that rule obsolete. And throw it out!

I know everyone likes a rule or five to fall back on, and I agree rules are good, but when exceptions far outnumber the examples of proper, effective usage, it is time to chuck the old rule.

RULES TO CHUCK

Here are a few rules that have been thoroughly discredited. And probably the dead giveaway that these rules are outmoded is the use of absolutes—"never" and "always." Exceptions almost always exist. You may have learned these rules in the class where you first learned the parts of speech and how to diagram sentences.

Always write in complete sentences. Every sentence must have a subject and a verb to make it complete. While knowing your subject and your verb is very good advice, and a great starting point, there are times when you'll want to write a sentence—probably for emphasis—in which you'll omit the subject because it's understood. And because repeating the subject again and again is very monotonous for the reader. It makes for boring reading. So don't do it. But carefully pick your exceptions, so you don't end up with staccato prose that reads like a tweet.

Never begin a sentence with a conjunction. Well, you'll notice in the preceding sentences I've already fractured that one. While you don't want to overuse this technique, you may start a sentence with a conjunction when you want to transition to your next point. It can work as a bridge—and a very effective one. And it can be very helpful in creating continuity in your prose.

Always use the active voice; never use the passive voice. This advice is almost always given to business writers. Here again, the rule is a very good one. It's often useful, and usually the best approach for the business writer. But there are those times when you will want to emphasize what is being acted on, and for that situation it's best to use the passive voice. And sometimes you'll just want to change things up so readers' eyes don't glaze over with the monotonous march of simple declarative sentences in the active voice. For variety, or to highlight the thing being acted on, the passive voice is what you'll want to use. Sure, you'll use this only infrequently, but it's an effective tool.

Never write in the first person when writing for business. This rule has its roots in academia, where the scientific community still usually writes more formally and in the third person. But writing in the first person is usually the best practice for the informal business communication. Even when you want to avoid the first person in a more formal document, you may want to first write it in the first person and then rewrite, removing the *I*s. This will help ensure that your writing is approachable for the reader.

Never end a sentence with a preposition. This rule has long been discredited because following it often makes for clumsy, awkward sentences. It simply isn't the way we talk to each other. Definitely, do end a sentence with a preposition when it's the most natural and clear way to express yourself. A preposition is a perfectly fine thing to end a sentence with.

Never address the reader directly when writing the business communication. This is a silly rule for the business writer because there are so many communications for which this is the whole point. Imagine, for example, writing an instruction manual, a personnel manual, or even an email without addressing the reader.

Never use contractions. I think almost every business writer has discarded this old canon in favor of making his writing more colloquial and approachable for the reader. Even for formal business writing, contractions are often the best choice. Give up stuffy for approachable.

Always use the simplest words; write to an eighth-grade level. There's an old formula (one of three, actually) that still floats out there called the "fog count." It was developed by the military in an effort to make military technical material easier for enlistees to understand.

Taking this rule to heart—if it can indeed be considered a rule—we'd be writing in one, two, and three syllables, instead of using the best words and the rich English vocabulary to make our prose both readable and inviting. It's safe to say, however, that government documents could certainly stand editing for easier reading. That's a fact that both President Carter and President Clinton tried to emphasize through legislation.

The grain of truth here is that to puff up what you are writing with four- and five-syllable words so you sound distinguished doesn't promote ease of reading and understanding. And that approach won't endear you to your readers. So strive to make your writing inviting, easy to understand, and concise. Write for your audience in the terms they will understand. And let the syllable count fall where it will.

Never split an infinitive. From about 1850 to 1925, many grammarians decided that separating the *to* from the principal verb in the infinitive verb form just shouldn't be done. So they instituted this silly rule, which lived a long and awkward life. Although the rule began to die shortly after 1925, it can still be found lurking in textbooks here and there. As Bill Walsh, copy chief at *The Washington Post*, points out in his book *The Elephants of Style*, "I know of no usage authorities who [now] believe that split infinitives are always wrong, but I take a more extreme position than most: More often than not, in my opinion, infinitives are better split."

So if you wish to effectively write the way most people talk, hear, and understand, it's perfectly fine to place the modifier next to the word it modifies. In fact, it avoids confusion and promotes understanding—and isn't that what you're trying to achieve? Put the adverb between the *to* and the principal verb, if that works best. In other words, split away if the result is a more effective sentence.

It's important to remember we're going for clarity in writing. Contorting a sentence just to avoid splitting *to* from the principal verb can entirely change your meaning, and it can make for some confusing prose. Here are a few examples:

WRITE CLEARLY	NOT CLUMSILY
to effectively *move* stock	*to move* effectively stock; *to move* stock effectively [the second is much better than the first choice]
we expect *to* more than *triple* profits	we expect *to triple* profits more than
to seamlessly *implement* the change	*To implement* the change seamlessly; *to implement* seamlessly the change
we decided *to* actually *enforce* the law	we decided *to enforce* actually the law; we decided *to enforce* the law actually

Notice that it works best to place the modifier closest to the word it modifies, even if it's immediately after the word.

RULES TO WRITE BY

There are a few simple rules that will keep your business writing from wandering into a grammatical quagmire:

1. *Make sure your subject and verb are in tune with each other.* Note that I have two subjects, or a *compound subject*—"subject" and "verb"—joined by "and," so my verb must be "are" for a plural subject, not "is" for a singular subject. If I had joined the subjects by "or" or "nor," I would use a singular verb form, "is."

When in doubt, do a little detective work and analyze your subject(s). Sometimes you may want to change things up and have the subject follow the verb in the sentence. This is called an inverted sentence. Ask yourself: *What is the subject?*

- Of particular concern *are* the *projections* for production next week and the following week.

The subject is *projections,* so we need the plural *are.*

2. *A collective noun used as a single subject usually takes a singular verb.* Examples include *committee, department, management, audience, crowd, cast, gang, fleet,* and *jury.*

- The *committee is* in session.
- The *department meets* at 2:00 p.m.

But when you want to note individuals in the group or more than one part of the group, use a plural verb:

- The *committee were* divided over the issue of pay increases.

But for ease of reading, instead of the following:

- The *department weren't* in agreement

state:

- The *department members weren't* in agreement.

Always give your sentences the "hearing" test. If a sentence doesn't sound right, rewrite it.

3. *Use a singular verb with indefinite pronouns.* Indefinite pronouns include *someone, somebody, anyone, each, either, everybody, everyone, anybody, anyone, anything, neither, nobody, no one, everything,* and *something.*

- *Nobody was* paid.
- *Each* of the employees *has* to apply.

4. Use a singular verb with plural nouns when you intend a singular meaning. Examples include *economics, physics, statistics, news, politics,* and *academics.*

- The *economics* of the decision *is* still the same.
- *Politics is* a contact sport.

But when you intend a plural meaning, use a plural verb:

- The *economics* of the plan *are* unacceptable.

5. Plural nouns in a title or company name, or plural words used as one category or unit, take a singular verb.

- *Lehman Brothers is* a good example.
- *A Tale of Two Cities is* arguably Dickens's best work.
- *Accrued assets is* the best category for that.

6. *When* who, which, *and* that *are subjects, they are called* relative pronouns, *and they have* antecedents, *or nouns or pronouns to which they refer.* When a relative pronoun is the subject of a subordinate (or dependent) clause, it takes a verb that agrees with its antecedent.

- Take the red-handled *tool that is* labeled "Install."

7. *When a pronoun is a bit sneaky, or ambiguous, because it could refer to more than one noun or antecedent in the sentence, rewrite the sentence to clear things up.*

- When Jim placed part A on the assembly line, *it* vibrated.

What does *it* refer to, the part or the assembly line? Rewrite:

- Part A vibrated when Jim placed *it* on the assembly line.

8. *Make sure your pronoun after* than *or* as *is correct.*

- I believe the boss likes you more *than me.*

Is this correct, or should the sentence read: I believe the boss likes you more *than I*? Reconstruct the sentence for meaning to be sure the pronoun following *than* is correct:

- I believe the boss likes you more *than* he likes *me*.

Me is correct. But to make things crystal clear for the reader, use the reconstructed sentence.

Do the same when you use *as*:

- Jim likes calculus *as* much as *I*.

Or is it:

- Jim likes calculus *as* much as *me*?

Reconstructed, the sentence is

- Jim likes calculus *as* much as *I* do.

I is correct. But, again, to be sure the sentence is clear to the reader, use the reconstructed sentence. Don't leave it to the reader to supply the "understood" verb.

9. *Use* who *and* whom *correctly.* This trips up some of the most proficient business writers. In fact, this rule is so often broken that it is often overlooked. (And some say current usage will soon change the rule altogether.) Still, be safe and get it right. You might just get the boss *who* is a stickler for correct grammar.

The first step in using the correct form is to decide whether the pronoun is the acting subject or the object of the action or verb. *Who* is equal to *he*, and *whom* is equal to *him*. *Who* (*he*) refers to the subject of the sentence or clause; *whom* (*him*) receives the action.

Do your detective work and reconstruct the sentence. Which is correct?

- Eddie Frank is the candidate *whom* we believe will be hired.
- Eddie Frank is the candidate *who* we believe will be hired.

Reconstructed correctly to find the answer, the sentence is:

- ... *who [he]* will be hired.

Take "we believe" out of the equation.

10. *Use subjective, objective, and possessive pronouns correctly.* Subjective pronouns are *I, you, he, she, it, we,* and *they.* Objective pronouns are *me, you, him, her, it, us,* and *them.* (Yes, *you* and *it* are on both lists.) Possessive pronouns are *my, your, his, her, its, our,* and *their.* (Possessive pronouns are always clear because of their use.)

Your detective work here will be to reconstruct the sentence to learn if the pronoun is the subject or the object. Writers usually get tangled up when there are multiple subjects or objects. Which is correct?

- Dan and *me* will make the presentation.
- Dan and *I* will make the presentation.

If you take Dan out of the equation, it's clear that *I* is correct.

Since objective pronouns are the objects of the action, which is correct?

- He came to my office to see *I*.
- He came to my office to see *me*.

Me is, of course, correct because it's the object of the action.

11. *Make sure your point of view is consistent.* You may write in the first person—*I, me, my, mine, we, our,* and *us*; the second person—*you, your,* and *yours*; or the third person—*he, she, him, her, his, hers, they, them, their,* and *theirs.* But be sure to maintain a consistent point of view throughout your communication.

- *I* will email the report later today. (Written in the first person.)
- *You* must email the report later today. (Written in the second person.)
- *He* will email the report later today. (Written in the third person.)

Don't shift points of view in the middle of your communication.

- *Department heads* should do production planning at 7:00 a.m. because *your* schedule is open at that time.

Wrong because *heads* is plural and *your* is singular.

- *Department heads* should do production planning at 7:00 a.m. because *their* schedule is open at that time.

This is correct because both *heads* and *their* are plural.

12. *Make sure appositives agree with the noun or pronoun they serve.* Appositives are words or phrases that give information about nouns or pronouns, but aren't essential to the sentence. Which is correct?

- The sales managers, Ted and *me*, could not agree on a new strategy.
- The sales managers, Ted and *I*, could not agree on a new strategy.

Do your detective work. By taking Ted out of the mix, you have:

- . . . *I* could not agree . . .

This same kind of sleuthing will help you determine the cases for subject complements (subjective-case pronouns that usually follow *be, am, is, are, was, were, being,* or *been* and rename or describe the subject). It will also help you decide whether to use *we* or *us* before a noun. Warning: sometimes the correct answer will sound "off," and if it does, the best approach is to rewrite the sentence.

Which is correct?

- During the committee meeting, Harry finally admitted that the prankster was *he*.
- During the committee meeting, Harry finally admitted that the prankster was *him*.

Reconstructing, you find, "*He* was the prankster." So *he* is correct. But you may want to rewrite the sentence to read:

- During the committee meeting, Harry finally admitted that *he* was the prankster.

Try this example:

- *Us* committee members came to an agreement.
- *We* committee members came to an agreement.

You'll find that *we* is correct when you reconstruct: "*we* came to an agreement."

13. *Know how the various verb forms work.* Sometimes verbs act up in a sentence. Instead of taking their verb roles, with a little adjustment they become verbals: participles (present or past), gerunds, and infinitives. Knowing how each works will help you write more effectively.

A participle can be formed by adding *-ing* (present) or *-ed* or *-d* (past). It may act as an adjective; if so, it answers the questions, What kind of? and Which one?

- *Rising* costs were the result of that decision: The *revised* estimates came in too high.
- The management team, *excited* over the new acquisition, announced it on Twitter.

In the first sentence, *rising* answers the question, What kind of costs? and *revised* answers the question, Which estimates? In the second sentence, *excited* answers the question, What kind of team?

A gerund is a verb with an -ing ending that acts as a noun; it names a person, place, or thing.

- *Exercising* during break will increase your energy and stamina.
- *Electing* a new chairman of the board is the next step toward better leadership.

In both sentences, the -*ing* ending turns the verbs into nouns.

An infinitive is a verb preceded by *to,* which usually acts as a noun, but may also take the form of an *adjective* or *adverb.*

- *To succeed* is the goal. (*To succeed* is a noun.)
- We decided *to fire* John. (*To fire* is an adverb that modifies *decided.*)
- Ted was the first person from our group *to graduate.* (*To graduate* is an adjective modifying *person.*)

Just to confuse you, once in a while the *to* in the infinitive may be dropped, but it's still an infinitive. Dissecting your sentences—or diagramming them—to expose the role of all the words will help you determine how each word is acting. When in doubt, do a bit of detective work; it becomes easier with practice. For example:

- Please help me *count* the votes.

Here *count* means the same as *to count*; the *to* has been omitted.

And this brings us all the way back to that tired and outmoded old rule about splitting infinitives. Again, split them when it makes your meaning clearer and your sentence more concise. Infrequently, when it sounds better, omit the *to.*

14. *Make sure your adjectives are well placed.* Usually the clearest construction places adjectives immediately before the nouns they modify.
Adjectives can also work as subject complements following linking verbs—usually a form of *to be*: *be, am, is, are, was, were, being,* and *been.*

- Work is therapeutic. (*Therapeutic* modifies *work.*)

Other verbs may invite an adjective that describes the subject, too. Some examples are *feel, taste, look,* and *appear.* If the word describes the subject, it is an adjective; if it describes the verb, it is an adverb (often ending in -*ly*). Know which you are using.

- The boss looked *skeptical*. (*Skeptical* is an adjective modifying *boss*.)
- The boss looked *skeptically* at the expense report. (*Skeptically* is an adverb modifying *looked*.)

15. ***Know your adverbs.*** The work of adverbs is to modify verbs, adjectives, and other adverbs. Eliminate those that entangle a sentence and that diffuse the impact. Effective adverbs answer the questions *when, where, how,* or *why?* They also answer the questions, Under what conditions? How often? or, To what degree? They are often easy to spot because they usually end in *-ly*. Place them as close to the word they modify as possible to keep your meaning clear.

Adjectives often suffer from misidentification and are improperly used as adverbs, particularly in conversation. So when you write, get it right: know what the adverb does and what it modifies. Which of the following is correct?

The chance of recovering lost production looks *near* impossible.
The chance of recovering lost production looks *nearly* impossible.

Nearly is correct because it modifies *impossible*.

Which of the following is correct?

- It was a job *well done*.
- He did a *good job*.

Both are correct. *Well* is correct because it modifies *done*. *Well* is an adverb; *good* is an adjective. *Good* is correct because it modifies *job*.

- Management was pleased that personnel had *done* so *good* on the skills test.

So, is this correct? No. It should be rewritten:

- Management was pleased that personnel had *done* so *well* on the skills test.

16. *Check the logic of your sentences.* Make sure that your subject and verb work together (make sense), that your sentences are coordinated, and that your comparisons hold up.

Faulty predication is the result of combining a subject and verb that don't make sense—the subject can't be or do the verb. Here are some examples.

- The new laboratory *analyzer assures* customers that they will be able to complete tests in less than thirty minutes.

Can the analyzer make customer assurances? No. Rewrite the sentence:

- *Baxter Corporation assures* customers that with the new analyzer they will be able to complete tests in less than thirty minutes.

Faulty coordination results if you join two clauses in an illogical way. Can you tell what's wrong with this example?

- I went to the interview, *yet* I left my résumé at home.

Yet makes the connection illogical. Rewrite:

- I went to the interview, *but* unfortunately I left my résumé at home.

Faulty coordination also results when you connect independent clauses of unequal importance.

- The price of the new model is $4,000, and it has a spare tire.

The price is more important; the spare tire is not equal in importance. You may rewrite this in a couple of ways:

- The price of the new model is $4,000, and that price includes a spare tire.

Or you could rewrite:

- The price of the new model is $4,000, which includes a spare tire.

Faulty comparisons occur when you compare two unlike people, places, or things. Decide what's wrong with these examples:

- The production slowdowns in June were more numerous than May.

What is being compared? The construction makes the sentence compare *slowdowns* to *May*. Rewrite the sentence:

- The production slowdowns in June were more numerous than the slowdowns in May.

Beware, too, of ambiguous comparisons that have more than one meaning or lend themselves to misinterpretation.

- Jim trusts production reports more than Susan.

Confusing? Rewrite:

- Jim trusts production reports more than Susan does.

Then we have absolute adjectives, which are words that cannot be compared. Here are some words you should not use in comparisons:

perfect	square	unique	complete
circle	favorite	straight	vacant
permanent	flawless	pure	true
unanimous	empty	round	dead

- The solution would be *more perfect* if you added a catalyst.

Nothing can be "more perfect," so, for example, don't use *more, most, quite, rather, somewhat,* or *very* with an absolute adjective.

Faulty comparatives and superlatives make your sentences unravel. Most adjectives and adverbs come in three forms: the positive, the comparative, and the superlative. Use the comparative when you are comparing two things; use the superlative when you are comparing three or more. Here are some examples:

POSITIVE (one)	COMPARATIVE (two)	SUPERLATIVE (three or more)
good	better	best
bad	worse	worst
rich	richer	richest
fast	faster	fastest
deep	deeper	deepest
soft	softer	softest
careful	more careful	most careful
beautiful	more beautiful	most beautiful
late	later	latest

So, are the following sentences correct?

● Of the two models, model A performed *best*.

Correct? No. Because you are comparing two things, *better* is correct.

● Of the three applicants, John is the *more* qualified.

Correct? No. Because there are three, use *most*.

17. *Avoid writing in generalizations.* It signals a lack of research or just plain foggy thinking. And don't use those all-inclusive words like *everything, all, anyone, everyone, best, always, never, only,* and *none* unless you are sure the facts support your statement.

Limit (or eliminate) the use of superlatives like *greatest, best, most, least, sensational,* and *fabulous.*

● *Everyone* was *delighted* with the office party.

Correct? No. To know that, the writer would have had to interview every person attending the party and determined that each was delighted. Undoubtedly, someone was less than delighted. Rewrite:

● I spoke to a dozen employees attending the office party, and they all said they were enjoying themselves.
● *Everything* indicates the new model will be a great success.

This sentence smacks of a lack of research. Rewrite it to give real information:

- Just under 92 percent of the twenty people in the focus group rated the new model a 20 percent improvement over the old model.

18. *Beware the non sequitur.* Make sure you present a logical effect from a cause. A closely related problem is a sentence that implies that what appears first caused what appears after (*post hoc, ergo propter hoc*).

- Production line A ran a full eight hours; therefore, the number of produced high-quality, completed units will be way up.

While this may be true, it also may not. It doesn't necessarily follow that running a full eight hours produces more high-quality completed units.

- We have eighty applications; therefore, we will find the right candidate.

Well, maybe not. The applicant pool could be a complete misfit.

19. *Check your writing to be sure you don't include a false (fallacious) dilemma, which presents only two alternatives, when there are more than two.*

- Employees may either appear at work on time or call in sick.

Actually, employees have several other options: they may take a personal day, use a vacation day, or arrange with their supervisor for a substitute if they will be late or absent.

20. *Eliminate circular reasoning from your writing.* A sentence that creates a circle of words without substance in the middle is a waste of effort.

- The Ebola epidemic is dangerous and may come to the United States.

While true, the second part of the sentence doesn't provide clarification about why the Ebola epidemic is dangerous.

21. *Eliminate the red herring.* It illogically cites an irrelevant issue or concern instead of the real one.

- Steve Jones was given the day off with pay to attend the conference, so I shouldn't be docked for the hours I was late for work.

Actually, Steve Jones's getting the day off has nothing to do with your being docked for being late.

22. *Eliminate sentence fragments.* A fragment is a series of words that lacks the three essential ingredients of a complete sentence: (1) a subject; (2) a predicate (verb); and (3) a complete thought. Don't let fragments show up in what you write. Sleuth your writing to make sure all your sentences have a subject and a verb and are able to stand alone, expressing a complete thought.

To repair any fragments you turn up, rewrite the clause or phrase to include both a subject and a verb, or combine the fragment with another sentence. Are the following sentences or fragments?

- He quit.

Yes, this has a subject and a predicate or verb, and it expresses a complete thought.

- Determined to make the best decision from the options given.

No, this isn't a sentence because there is no subject. Who determined? This can be easily corrected by adding a subject like "He" or a name at the beginning.

But fragments are useful in some business writing. For the very informal email message, you may use a fragment in a response to, say, a multiple choice question. When writing a stepped procedure, you may want to include a list of bulleted items (fragments); or, infrequently, you may use a fragment in your writing for emphasis. I'd stress here *infrequently*. (All of these uses are acceptable only when you are sure the reader will understand. To be safe, it's better to write in complete sentences.)

23. *Tame the run-on sentence.* I've saved the thorniest and most common problem of the business writer until last. But avoiding run-ons isn't as tough as you might imagine and becomes easier with practice. Your reader's eyes will glaze over and he'll quickly abandon your opus if the sentences are stuffed with long trains of cascading ideas that fall in long paragraphs on the screen or page without so much as a comma to slow things down. (Pretty hefty sentence right there.)

The first kind of run-on sentence we'll tackle is the fused sentence. It contains two or more complete thoughts but lacks the necessary punctuation between the thoughts to make them easy to understand.

The secret to taming this beast? Simplify, simplify, simplify; or punctuate, punctuate, punctuate. This is the only way to get your sentence under control and keep your reader reading. How would you tame this run-on?

- The new mechanical air conditioner will be mounted over the boardroom it will operate independently of the central air-conditioning system.

Can you see where one independent clause ends and the next begins?

There are two ways to tame this run-on sentence: (1) insert a comma and a coordinating conjunction (*and, but, or, nor, for, so, yet*) between the independent clauses; or (2) insert a semicolon (or sometimes a colon or a dash) between the clauses.

Let's try it.

- The new mechanical air conditioner will be mounted over the boardroom, *and* it will operate independently of the central air-conditioning system.

I could also have used *but* if I wanted a different meaning. Or I could have made this change:

- The new mechanical air conditioner will be mounted over the boardroom; it will operate independently of the central air-conditioning system.

What a difference a tiny bit of punctuation makes. When the punctuation is missing, we have a fused mess; when the punctuation is in place, we have a perfectly readable sentence.

The second kind of run-on sentence is more common in business writing. It is the run-on sentence sprinkled with commas, called the comma splice, or the comma fault. This sentence has two complete thoughts that are spliced together by just a comma and no coordinating conjunction. Here's an example:

- The new mechanical air conditioner will be mounted over the boardroom, it will operate independently of the central air-conditioning system.

See the problem?
Here's another one:

- All applications are due by Friday noon, late applications will not be considered.

In other comma splices, there is a comma and a joining word, such as *however,* but there is no coordinating conjunction. So how do you fix the problem? Select the best of four ways:

1. Insert a comma and a coordinating conjunction between the independent clauses.
2. Insert a semicolon (or, if appropriate, a colon or a dash) between the independent clauses.
3. Divide the run-on sentence into two sentences.
4. Rewrite the sentence, making one of the independent clauses into a dependent one.

Here's the first sentence again:

- The new mechanical air conditioner will be mounted over the boardroom, *but* it will operate independently of the central air-conditioning system. (I've used a comma and a coordinating conjunction, *but.*)

- The new mechanical air conditioner will be mounted over the boardroom; it will operate independently of the central air-conditioning system. (I've used a semicolon.)
- The new mechanical air conditioner will be mounted over the boardroom. It will operate independently of the central air-conditioning system. (I've made two sentences.)
- The new mechanical air conditioner will be mounted over the boardroom, *though* it will operate independently of the central air-conditioning system. (I've created an independent and subordinate clause, and I've inserted a comma.)

TIPS

- Know your personal pronoun cases.

Subjective Case	Objective Case	Possessive Case
I	me	my
we	us	our
you	you	your
he/she/it	him/her/it	his/her/its
they	them	their

- Go for short, active sentences and short paragraphs to keep your readers reading.
- When you can't easily untangle the run-on sentence, rewrite it into a simpler, reader-friendly, and complete form.
- If in doubt about your sentence, reduce it to its simplest form: the subject and the verb (predicate); then figure out how the rest of the modifiers fit into the picture and place them as close as possible to the word or phrase they modify.

10

Misused, Confused, and Abused Words

On my first assignment to report on a trip to Mexico, I interviewed the colorful musicians and dancers at a resort and wrote about the wonderful "flamingo music." OK, it was undoubtedly the Spanglish and my hearing, but I'd never seen or heard the word "flamenco." When the editor read my piece, he called me and laughed heartily. He knew the difference between those pink plastic bird ornaments that festoon some neighborhood lawns and the art of dancing in that certain south-of-the-border way. Thank goodness.

But in business, if you get the word or its usage wrong, you may not have a sympathetic editor, or boss, who catches the mistake and corrects it before it goes viral. And there may be very serious, undesirable consequences.

Using the correct word and using words correctly are the marks of a business writer who is going places. Check yourself on these words, which are commonly misused, confused, or abused in business writing.

a or an   *A* is *an* article that precedes a consonant sound; the article *an* precedes a vowel sound.
It's *a* historical event—awarding *an* honorary degree. (Check *honorary* and you'll hear the soft *o* sound.)

about or at about   Omit *at*.
He arrived *about* 8:00 a.m.
Or, if you want to be precise:
He arrived *at* 8:00 a.m.

accept or **except**   To *accept* is to consent, or believe; to *except* is to exclude.

He *accepted* the changes to the report *except* for item 1.a.

acute or **chronic**   *Acute* means severe or sharp; *chronic* means long-lasting.

We have had a *chronic* need for more inventory, but it has suddenly become *acute*.

adapt or **adopt**   To *adapt* is to change; to *adopt* is to take up, start to use, or follow.

We can easily *adapt* to daylight savings time.

The question is: Will we *adopt* the amendment as written?

adverse or **averse**   *Adverse* means unfavorable, contrary, or hostile and is generally used to refer to situations, conditions, or events; *averse* is having a strong feeling of opposition, repugnance, or antipathy and is generally used to refer to people.

He is *averse* to initiating the new uniform policy until the *adverse* condition of no air-conditioning in the plant is corrected.

advice or **advise**   *Advice* is the noun; *advise* is the verb.

I *advise* you to take my *advice* and cancel the contract.

affect or **effect (affective** or **effective)**   To *affect* (verb) is to have an influence; an *effect* (noun) is the result.

If you want to *affect* a change in the resulting *effect*, use your influence with the committee.

Much less common is using *affect* (pronounced with emphasis on the first syllable) as a noun to describe a psychological condition. *Effect* as a verb means to bring about.

Affective is usually used only to describe emotions, as in "seasonal *affective* disorder." *Effective* is used to describe what is working well, is forceful, powerful, or capable.

He is an *effective* leader.

(But this word is a bit tired; try not to overuse it.)

aggravate or **annoy**   To *aggravate* is to make worse, or exaggerate; to *annoy* is to irritate.

He's trying to *annoy* you, so don't *aggravate* the situation by responding.

aid or **aide**   *Aid* is what you give; *aide* is a helper.

I'll ask my *aide* to make sure *aid* arrives tomorrow.

all ready or **already**   *All ready* means everything is ready; *already* is an adverb meaning prior to a specified time, or before now.

I *already* have the lunch *all ready.*

all right or **alright**   It's still two words.

all together or **altogether**   *All together* means all at once, or simultaneously; *altogether* means entirely, or wholly.

Please sing *all together*; it will make an *altogether* beautiful harmony.

allude or **elude**   To *allude* is to refer to indirectly; to *elude* is to evade, avoid, or escape.

She *alluded* to the fact that the new policy had been approved.

He *eluded* detection by exiting the side door.

allusion or **illusion**   *Allusion* is an indirect or passing reference; *illusion* is something wrongly perceived or deceptive to the senses.

Dick's statement about the crash was a veiled *allusion* to last year's computer failure.

The silhouette gives the *illusion* of a much more expensive car.

a lot or **alot** or **allot**   It's still two words.

altar or **alter**   An *altar* is an elevated place for religious offerings; to *alter* is to change.

He was left at the *altar.*

Please *alter* your approach.

alternate or **alternative**   *Alternate* means every other one in a series; *alternative* means one of two choices.

We were left with no *alternative*; we had to use the *alternate* plan.

alumni, **alumnae**, **alumnus**, **alum**, or **alumna**   Who knew graduating could be so complicated? A male graduate is an *alumnus*; a female graduate is an *alumna*; several female graduates are *alumnae*; several male graduates or several male and female graduates are *alumni*; and they may all be informally called *alum* (or *alums*).

among or **between**   *Among* is used with three or more; *between* is used with two.
Among the dozen candidates, two were selected.
Between the two finalists, John was the better candidate.

and I or **and me**   *I* does the action; *me* receives it. Take the other person (or element) out of the sentence, and you'll find the correct usage.
James *and I* will make the presentation. (*I* will make the presentation.)
He called on James and *me* to help. (He called on *me*.)

antennas or **antennae**   *Antennae* belong to insects; *antennas* are used on cars and equipment.

anticipate or **expect**   You prepare for something if you *anticipate* it; you may not if you *expect* it.
I *expect* it may rain.
I *anticipate* a change in the weather, so I'll bring in the new signage.

anticlimactic or **anti-climactic**   No hyphen is correct.

anybody or **any body**   Use *anybody* when you mean any one person; *any body* is a body.
Any body type can successfully wear this dress.
Is *anybody* ready for lunch?

anymore or **any more**   One word is correct. Use it for making a negative statement.
We don't offer that model *anymore*.

anywhere from or **about**   Use *about* to denote approximately; eliminate *anywhere from* when you want to indicate approximately or from one point to another.

He will arrive *about* 3:00 p.m.
The cost will be *between* [not *anywhere from*] $1.34 and $1.52.

appraise or **apprise**   *Appraise* is a verb that means to assess the value or quality of something; *apprise* is a verb that means to inform or tell.
Please *appraise* the items, then *apprise* me of your findings.

as or **like**   Use *as* when the object of the comparison has its own verb.
David works *as* Bill does.
Use *like* to make a direct comparison.
David works *like* Bill.

as good, **as to whether**, or **as yet**   Cut unnecessary words; use *good, whether,* or *yet.*

as soon as or **will**   Use *as soon as* when something is a possibility, *will* when it's a certainty.
The shipment may arrive *as soon as* tomorrow.
Jim said the shipment *will* arrive tomorrow.

assume or **presume**   While some dictionaries use these interchangeably, use *assume* when you have no facts, *presume* when you have some.
Don't *assume* you know the policy if you haven't read the employee manual.
I *presume* he will be here because he said he would.

assure, **ensure**, or **insure**   To *assure* means to offer assurance; to *ensure* means to make sure; to *insure,* while it means to *ensure,* is more correctly used to mean to *have insurance.*
To *ensure* the safety of our customers, we have made our seat belts fail-safe.
We *assure* you the seat belts are fail-safe.
To *insure* your family against a vacation medical emergency, see the policies on pages 20 to 52.

attorneys or **lawyers**   A person with a law degree is a *lawyer*; a person who acts on behalf of someone else is his *attorney*.

He is a *lawyer* with a degree from the University of Chicago.

He is our corporate *attorney*.

bad or **badly**   *Bad* is an adjective and *badly* is an adverb. The exceptions are what trip people up. When the word modifies an action verb, use *badly*; when it modifies a form of a linking verb—*be, is, was, did*—use *bad*.

We *badly* need to get this order filled today.

What Susan did was *bad* enough; what she said was worse.

Maybe more simply, when you're writing about how you feel, use *bad*. When you're writing about how someone did something or reacted or performed, use *badly*.

bare or **bear**   *Bare* is "without" (as in naked); to *bear* is to have, display, support, or endure.

Please *bear* this in mind: the *bare* facts suggest a cover-up.

because of or **due to**   Use *because of* when you mean "as a result of"; *due to* implies something that was expected or owed.

Because of the delay in shipping, there will be no delivery today.

The shipment was *due to* arrive before noon.

bemused or **amused**   *Bemused* means bewildered or perplexed; it doesn't mean *amused*.

besides or **beside**   *Besides* means "in addition to"; *beside* means "by the side of."

Besides the four of you, we will have John standing *beside* Jeremy.

both agree or **they agree**   Don't improperly use *both* when writing about two people; use *they agree*.

breath or **breathe**   A *breath* is one; to *breathe*, you inhale and exhale a number of times (it's the act of breathing).

Take a *breath* before you continue; then *breathe* normally, and you'll be fine.

can or **may**   *Can* refers to the ability to do something; *may* asks permission or states a possibility or hope.

I *can* walk two miles on my lunch hour, but I *may* just walk around the block.

cannot, am not, do not, or **is not** (and all the other "nots")   *Cannot* is one word; the rest are two.

capital or **capitol**   *Capitol* is the legislative building (for the federal one in Washington, D.C., use a capital *C*), meaning the seat of government; *capital* is money and all other references.

carat, caret, carrot, or **karat**   *Carat* is the unit of weight of precious stones, metals, and pearls; it's the British spelling for *karat*. *Caret* is an editorial mark (∧) to indicate the place at which to insert something; and *carrot* is the much-maligned vegetable children resist eating.

cellphone or **cell phone**   There's still disagreement, but *cellphone* has now been sanctioned the proper word by virtue of common use, though many purists still object.

cite, sight, or **site**   *Sight* is vision; to *cite* is to note a specific source (especially in your writing); and a *site* is a location, physical or on the Internet.

Please *cite* your source when quoting from a Web *site*.

Your *sight* can suffer if you spend too much time online.

coarse or **course**   Something is *coarse* if it is unrefined or rough in texture; to take a *course* is to take a route or direction (or a unit of study).

His speech was *coarse*. But his knowledge of the *course* material was outstanding.

complement or **compliment**   To *complement* is to complete or bring to perfection; to *compliment* is to express praise or admiration.

The handbag is the perfect *complement* to that suit, and Susan will certainly receive many *compliments* on the outfit.

continued or **postponed**   A court trial may be *continued,* but when your business meeting is put off until another day, use *postponed.*

could of or **could have**   *Could have* is correct; don't write *could of, would of, should of, might of,* or *may of.*

council or **counsel**   A *council* is an advisory or legislative body of people; to give *counsel* is to give advice.
The *council counseled* him on his rights in the matter.

countries, states, and **cities**   In constructing a sentence, make consistent comparisons. Don't say, for example, "We have offices in Detroit, Phoenix, and Colorado." Name either the cities or the states, and do the same for countries.

data is or **data are**   *Data* is plural, but its widespread use as singular is changing the rule.

definite or **definitive**   *Definite* means clearly stated or decided; *definitive* means done or reached decisively and with authority.
Although we found some *definite* weaknesses in the committee's subpoints, the decision will stand as the *definitive* policy for the future.

defuse or **diffuse**   To *defuse* is to remove the fuse from a bomb or reduce the danger or tension in a situation; to *diffuse* is to disperse randomly.

dessert or **desert**   To *desert* is to leave, fail at a critical moment, or run away from. It also means dry and barren. And *dessert* is that sweet treat at the end of a meal. (Think of the sugar as adding an extra *s.*)

different from or **different than**   To write it correctly, use *different from* when you are comparing and *different than* when you mean unlike.

dilemma   A *dilemma* is a difficult choice between two or more (usually undesirable) alternatives. Don't use it to mean a problem.
Our *dilemma* was this: lay off twenty-five workers or require seventy-five employees to go from full-time to part-time.

disassemble or dissemble   To *disassemble* means to dismantle; to *dissemble* means to conceal one's true motives.

disburse or disperse   *Disburse* means to give out (especially money); *disperse* means to scatter.

discreet or discrete   To be *discreet* is to be careful or circumspect, while *discrete* means separate.
I trust you will be *discreet* and not share what you have heard in this meeting. We will treat all such infractions as a *discrete* category.

disinterested, indifferent, or uninterested   Use *disinterested* when you mean impartial, *indifferent* or *uninterested* when you mean not interested in.

divided into or composed of   Use *divided into* when you mean separated into parts; use *composed of* when you mean consists of.
Divide the production employees *into* two shifts *composed of* 125 workers in each group.

dual or duel   *Dual* means having two parts or aspects; a *duel* is a contest or fight.
We will offer *dual* choices for the event instead of *dueling* over which to feature.

each and every, every one, or everyone   Write *every one*, not *each and every*, when you mean each unless you are using a direct quote. *Everyone* is the pronoun equal to *everybody*.

emigrate or immigrate   *Emigrate* means to exit one's place of residence or country; *immigrate* means to enter into a country.
Children and their parents want to *emigrate* from Central American countries and *immigrate* into the United States.

envelop or **envelope**   *Envelop*, a verb, means to wrap up, cover, or surround; *envelope*, a noun, is the paper container for a letter. But the *phrase* "push the envelope" means to extend the limits of what is possible.

everyday or **every day**   Use *everyday* to mean happening daily or routinely; use *every day* when you mean every single day.

expedient or **expeditious**   *Expedient* means doing something conveniently or practically; *expeditious* means doing something efficiently.

It may be the most *expedient* way to operate, but it's definitely not the most *expeditious*.

farther or **further**   *Farther* means a greater physical distance; *further* means beyond in an abstract sense, or in time or quantity. The distinction is fading, but use *further* when writing about ideas and opinions.

To the point of economy, the distance model C will travel on one gallon of fuel is five miles *farther* than model B will travel. *Further* testing will be needed.

faze or **phase**   *Faze* means to disturb or disconcert (someone); *phase* is a unit or period of time.

He wasn't *fazed* by the change in the assembly *phase* of the process.

fewer or **less**   Use *fewer* when you write about people or countable things (and only with plural nouns), *less* or *lesser* to modify mass nouns that can't be counted.

The new product will appeal to *fewer* customers because it has *less* design appeal.

flammable or **inflammable**   These words are commonly confused, and the difference is an issue of safety. *Inflammable* means combustible, but *flammable* is used on vehicles carrying combustible products.

flaunt or **flout**   *Flaunt* means to display ostentatiously; *flout* means to openly disregard.
Flaunting his red and orange outfit, he *flouted* the dress code for the occasion.

flesh or **flush**   To *flesh* out is to add weight or substance to an incomplete outline or form; to *flush* out is to cleanse or clean out. It can also mean when the skin becomes red and hot.

flounder or **founder**   *Flounder* can be a fish, but as a verb it means to struggle or move with difficulty. *Founder,* as a noun, means a manufacturer of cast metal or the person who establishes an institution or a business; as a verb, *founder* means to fail completely or to sink.
Talks *floundered* on a number of issues, including a new health insurance plan and pay increases, but finally *foundered* on the issue of employee wage increases.

folk or **folks**   *Folk* is a collective noun (plural); *folks* is a colloquial form. Use *folk* in writing, if you must use it at all.

forego, forgo, or **foregone**   To *forego* is to go before; to *forgo* is to go without.
It's a *foregone* conclusion that he will *forgo* dessert.

foreword or **forward**   *Foreword* is the short introduction to a book; *forward* is toward the front, onward, or toward the future.
Read the *foreword* before moving *forward* in the book.

fortuitous or **fortunate**   *Fortuitous* is what happens by chance; to be *fortunate* is to be lucky or to experience good fortune.
It was a *fortuitous* meeting, which turned out to be *fortunate* for everyone.

free, for free, or **at no charge**   *Free* is an adverb that shouldn't be yoked with *for*. If you prefer not to use the naked word, substitute "at no charge."

fulsome, **full**, or **abundant**   *Fulsome* is an adjective, which means excessively flattering, though it is still sometimes used to mean abundant. To be safe, use *abundant* when you mean abundant and *full* when you mean full.

gauge or **gage**   *Gauge* is an instrument used for measuring; *gage* is a bit archaic, and means a pledge, especially a glove thrown down as a symbol to challenge another to a fight. *Gage* also has a nautical meaning, as in "weather gage."
We can *gauge* the veracity of the competition if we throw down the *gage* of a price war.

gay or **homosexual**   Both terms are now part of the language. Use them interchangeably.

good or **well**   To be *good* (an adjective) is to be desired or approved of, display moral virtue, or give pleasure; *well* (an adverb) means in a satisfactory or thorough manner.
It's a *good* thing he did *well* on the test.

gratuitous, **gratitude**, or **grateful**   *Gratuitous* is an adjective that means uncalled for, lacking good reason, or unwarranted. Don't use it to mean *gratitude*, a noun, which is the quality of being thankful, or the readiness to show appreciation for a kindness; and *grateful*, an adjective, means thankful, or feeling appreciation for a kindness.

hear or **here**   *Hear* is a verb, which means to receive sound with the ear; *here* is an adverb used to denote a time, place, or situation.
Did you *hear* that the meeting will take place *here?*

hoard or **horde**   *Horde* is a noun that means a huge crowd; *hoard* is a noun that means a stored-up supply. As a verb, to *hoard* means to gather up and store away.
A *horde* of customers waited for the store to open; they were intent on buying and *hoarding* the items on special.

hopefully, **I hope**, or **it is hoped**   *Hopefully*, an adverb, means in a hopeful manner. Use *it is hoped* or *I hope* when that's what you mean.

He waited *hopefully* for the announcement.
It is hoped that the change will take place by Friday.
I hope you will join us.

i.e. or e.g.   Don't confuse these. The abbreviation *i.e. (id est)* means that is, and what follows equals what has preceded it. Use *e.g. (exempli gratia,* for example) when you want to indicate that what follows is an example.

imply or infer   *Imply* is a verb denoting the speaker's words; listeners are left to *infer* from what is said.
He *implied* that all overtime would be canceled, but employees *inferred* that he referred only to shipping employees' overtime.

in or into   *In* means within or inside; *into* means moving from the outside to the inside.
Place the equipment *into* the capsule. When everything is *in*, we will seal it.

in box, in-box, or inbox   Common usage dictates that the two words are now one: *inbox*. Purists still prefer *in-box*.

in regard to, as regards, or in regards to   *In regard to* is often incorrectly written as *in regards to*. The phrase *as regards* is correct; but it's often best to strike the phrase entirely and start with the subject.

irregardless or regardless   *Irregardless* is incorrect. Write *regardless*.
Regardless of the weather, the program will start at 1:00 p.m.

isle or aisle   An *isle* is an island; an *aisle* is a corridor connecting one place to another.

its or it's   *It's* is a contraction that means it is; *its* is the possessive of something belonging to it.
It's time for the air conditioner to receive *its* routine maintenance.

lay or lie   *Lay* is a transitive verb that takes an object. The present, past, and past perfect tenses are *lay* (I *lay* my tools on the bench),

laid (I *laid* my tools on the bench), and *have laid* (I *have laid* my tools on the bench). *Lie* is an intransitive verb, which means it takes no direct object. The present, past, and past perfect tenses are *lie* (I *lie* down), *lay* (I *lay* down), and *have lain* (I *have lain* down).
Please *lay* your tools down and *lie* down for a rest.

lead or **led**   *Lead* is the present tense; *led* is the past tense.
He *led* the discussion yesterday, and Jack will *lead* it next week.

levee or **levy**   A *levee* is an embankment built to prevent the overflow of a river or canal; to *levy* is to impose a tax.

loan or **lend**   *Loan* is a noun; *lend* is the verb.
To make the *loan*, our bank will *lend* $45,000.

long-standing or **longtime**   Hyphenate *long-standing*; write *longtime* as one word.

loose or **lose**   *Loose* is the opposite of tight, and *lose* is the opposite of find.
We will *lose* this load if the strapping is too *loose*.

me, **myself**, or **I**   *I* is used only as a subject (like *she, he, we,* and *they*); *me* is the object (like *him, her, us,* and *them*); and *myself* is a reflexive pronoun, which you use when you are the object of your own action. (The exception is when you write, "I myself felt the punishment was severe.")

mitigate or **militate**   *Mitigate,* a verb, means to make something bad less severe; to *militate* (almost always used with *against*) is to try powerfully to prevent.
Let's *mitigate* the lack of wage increase by offering a bonus program. This will *militate* against a possible strike.

mould or **mold**   *Mould* is the British spelling; *mold* is the American. Both mean the form or frame for shaping something, or a form of fungus.

notable or **notorious**   *Notable* is an adjective, which means worthy of note, or remarkable; and *notorious* is an adjective used to mean famous or well-known because of its bad qualities or deeds.
He did *notable* work in exposing the *notorious* tactics of the competition.

on line or **online**   Current usage has become *online*.

pallet, palate, or **palette**   A *pallet* is a wooden platform or form; the *palate* is the roof of the mouth; and a *palette* is a thin board or slab on which an artist mixes colors.

panacea or **cure-all**   *Panacea* means *cure-all*. Don't use the word to mean a cure for a single thing.

passed, surpassed, or **past**   *Passed* is the verb, which means to have moved or caused to move; to have *surpassed* is to have exceeded; *past* is an adjective or noun that means last or the preceding time.
We *passed* by the storefront and noticed that the signage that was used for the *past* ten years has been removed.
Our sales *surpassed* last year's by 20 percent.

peak, peek, or **pique**   A *peak* is a projecting point or shape; to *peek* is to look quickly, usually in a furtive manner; and *pique* is a feeling of irritation or resentment, or can mean to stimulate.
Mr. Rowe's ire was *piqued* when he was told that employees had *peeked* at the production results, which showed a *peak* for the month of August.

per, as per, or **per se**   Eliminate these unnecessary and pompous words from your writing.

peremptory or **preemptive**   *Peremptory* means insisting on immediate attention or obedience; *preemptive* is action taken before an adversary can act.

perpetrate or **perpetuate**   To *perpetrate* something is to commit it; to *perpetuate* something is to keep something alive or going.

perquisite or **prerequisite** A *perquisite* is a special right or privilege because of one's position; a *prerequisite* is something required as a prior condition for something to happen.

perspective or **prospective** *Perspective* is a particular way of regarding something or a point of view. It can also be a two-dimensional drawing. *Prospective* is a future possibility or expectation.

peruse or **glance over** *Peruse* actually means to read or review something carefully; it doesn't mean to *glance over*. Use it correctly.

photogenic or **photographic** *Photogenic* means a person looks attractive in photographs; *photographic* means pertaining to photography.

pleaded or **pled** Use *pleaded* as the past-tense form. Don't use *pled*. He *pleaded* for a change in policy.

pore or **pour** *Pore* is a small opening in the skin, and also means the act of reading something intently; to *pour* is to flow or cause to flow in a steady stream.
The attorney is *poring* over the bylaws before he advises the board.
Please *pour* the coffee at 10:00 a.m.

PowerPoint, **power point**, or **Powerpoint** *PowerPoint* is the brand name of Microsoft's presentation software. Write it correctly as either *Microsoft PowerPoint* or *PowerPoint*.

practice or **practise** *Practise* is the British spelling; *practice* is the American spelling.

precede or **proceed** To *precede* is to come before; to *proceed* is to continue or go on.

prescribe or **proscribe** To *prescribe* is to command or recommend something; to *proscribe* someone or something is to outlaw him or it.

prevaricate or **procrastinate**   To *prevaricate* is to speak or act in an evasive way; to *procrastinate* is to put off doing something that needs to be done.

principle or **principal**   A *principle* is a fundamental truth or the foundation for a system of belief; *principal* is first in order of importance, main, or the person in charge. It also means capital sum.
The guiding *principle* of our investing strategy is that the *principal* should never be at great risk.

progeny or **prodigy**   *Progeny* are descendants or offspring of people, animals, or plants; a *prodigy* is a person, particularly a young person, endowed with exceptional abilities or talents.

quite or **quiet**   *Quite* means to a certain or fairly significant extent or degree; *quiet* means little or no noise.
It's *quite* necessary to maintain *quiet* in the patient wards.

real or **really**   *Real* is an adjective, which means actually existing as a thing or occurring in fact; *really* is an adverb, which means in actual fact, or very or thoroughly.
The *real* problem is proving that Jim is *really* innocent.

rein, **reign**, or **rain**   *Rein* as a noun is the strap used on a horse; as a verb, it means to control. To *reign*, the verb, is to rule over; as a noun, it is the period of time a ruler oversees a kingdom. *Rain* is that moisture that falls from the sky.
We will need to *rein* in the enthusiasm for the new model if we want to *reign* as sales kings of the standard model.
Rain is in the forecast.

reluctant or **reticent**   *Reluctant* is unwilling or disinclined to do something; *reticent* is not revealing one's feelings or thoughts readily.

set, **sit**, or **sat**   To *set* means to place something. It is a transitive verb that must have an object. *Sit* is an intransitive verb that doesn't need an object, and means to rest in an upright position; and *sat* is the past tense of *sit*.

Please *set* the drill down, *sit* down, and remain in the chair until you have *sat* there for five minutes.

stationery or **stationary**   An immovable object is *stationary*; *stationery* is the paper on which you write a letter.

supposed to or **suppose to**   Write *supposed to*; don't drop the *d*.

We are *supposed to* get the shipment today.

tack or **tact**   *Tack,* the noun, is a small nail; the verb means to attach or add. *Tact,* a noun, is diplomacy or skill in handling difficult situations.

than or **then**   *Than* is correct if you are introducing a second element for comparison; use *then* when you mean next or afterward.

Bob finished faster *than* I did, but *then,* during the next shift, we both fell off our beginning pace.

that or **which**   *That* introduces an essential clause; *which* introduces a nonessential clause. Use a comma before *which*.

It's the plan *that* offers the best solution.

The plan, *which* will be enacted on Friday, requires everyone's cooperation.

there, **their**, or **they're**   *There* means that place or that position; *their* means belonging to; and *they're* is the contraction for they are.

They're going to be enrolled in *their* training session, which will be held *there* in Houston.

till or **til**   Correct usage is *till*, which means *until*.

to, **too**, or **two**   *To* means in the direction; *too* means also; and *two* is the number.

To get your check, follow Ned to one of the *two* HR offices; he's collecting his check, *too*.

toward, **anyway**, or **afterward**   Do not attach *s* to these words.

treasurys or **treasuries**   U.S. Treasury securities are *Treasurys* for short, not *Treasuries*. The rule of adding *s* to proper nouns that end in *y* (Grammys, Emmys) is almost always correct. An exception is the Colorado Rockies.

troop or **troupe**   A *troupe* is a group of actors, dancers, or entertainers; a *troop* is any other group, like soldiers or Cub Scouts.

try and or **try to**   *Try to* is more formal, and *try and,* though usually correct, can sometimes sound awkward. Use *try to* for widest acceptance.

ultimate or **best**   *Ultimate* really means the last in a list of items, but it is routinely used to mean the *best*. Use *best* when you mean *best, ultimate* when you mean last on the list.

up to or **or more**   When used together, *up to or more,* results in a completely meaningless statement. Use real numbers, or don't use both.

use to or **used to**   *Use to* means to take, hold, or deploy; *used to* is the past tense. Don't write the past tense without the *d.*
I *used to* enjoy eating lunch near the fountain.

warrantee or **warranty**   A *warranty* is a legal assurance that something will perform a specified task or meet certain quality standards; a *warrantee* is the person who benefits from the *warranty.*

who or **whom**   *Who* is the subject; *whom* is the object of the action.
Who is calling? To *whom* shall I direct your call?

whose or **who's**   *Whose* means belonging to or associated with a person; *who's* is a contraction for who is.
The person *who's* assigned to clean up after the party will have to decide *whose* belongings were left in the room.

within or **in**   Use *within* when you mean inside a range from and to; use *in* whenever it works.

In four to seven days, we will receive the committee's changes; then the final draft will be written *within* the next six days.

your or **you're**   *Your* is the possessive of you, and *you're* is the contraction for you are.

You're going to need to clean *your* area before 5:00 p.m.

11

Business Writing Etiquette

Since the beginning of civilization, codes of conduct for human interaction have been written. Preceding the Bible's Golden Rule, which appears in the New Testament (Matthew 7:12) and instructs each person to treat every other person as he would like to be treated, much earlier instructions in the Old Testament include the Ten Commandments and the Book of Ecclesiastes, which even gives directions about table manners: "Eat as it becometh a man . . . And devour not, lest thou be hated."

The Talmud has rules for everything from self-control to licking the fingers. And the earliest Egyptian writings dating back as far as 2500 BCE encourage a code of conduct of striving for truthfulness, exercising self-control, and showing kindness toward others. The underpinnings of the code were the avoidance of conflict and the pursuit of justice.

During the Middle Ages in Europe, codes of conduct emanated from the royal and elite classes and were expressed in things like the knights' code of chivalry. While civility became expressed in a melding of manners with morals, the word *etiquette* is generally considered to have originated in France in connection with Louis XIV's seventeenth-century court at Versailles. According to Saint-Simon, a court observer, the king issued a decree that signs or "tickets" could be posted warning "keep within the *etiquettes*," or marked path. From this it is believed that the term grew to cover all codes or rules for conduct and deportment within court circles. The distinction became that etiquette is the set of exterior rules and manners are an expression of inner character.

In early American society, rules of etiquette were penned by George Washington, who at fourteen produced "Rules of Civility." William Penn, Benjamin Franklin, and many others also wrote rules for proper behavior as guides.

As society changed, so did the rules of etiquette. After World War I (1914–1918), as roles for women broadened, so did their rules of conduct. Emily Post is often credited with heralding that change, recording the new rules, and calling for higher standards of social conduct for the growing middle class with the publication of her book on the topic in 1922, *Etiquette in Society, in Business, in Politics and at Home.*

POLITICAL CORRECTNESS

Flash forward to the 1970s in the United States. We find the more sensitive and liberal of academic proponents beginning to insist that the code of kindness and consideration be more actively extended to all protected and disadvantaged classes—political, social, and economic. They took up the torch to eliminate the use of any speech, written word, or gesture that could be perceived as discriminatory, insulting, or injurious to anyone—especially in matters of race, gender, religion, ethnicity, age, or sexual orientation. This movement became labeled political correctness (PC) by people on the conservative side of the political spectrum.

The late 1980s and early 1990s saw the political-correctness movement grow, the debate between conservatives and liberals polarize, and the pendulum sometimes swing wildly to the extremes. In efforts to define exactly what terms are objectionable, tomes were penned and then revised. And revised. And revised. In politically correct speech, "Indian" became "Native American," and later "Oriental" became "Asian." Scores of words like "feminine" and "codger" quickly became taboo. And cries to remove those who violated politically correct speech were aimed at radio and television personalities like Jimmy the Greek, Howard Cosell, Chief Illiniwek, and Jackie Mason.

The New York Times reported that President George H. W. Bush's commencement speech at the University of Michigan in May 1991 expressed the conservative view when he said:

> The notion of political correctness declares certain topics, certain expressions, even certain gestures, off-limits. What began as a crusade for civility has soured into a cause of conflict and even censorship.

The late William Safire devoted his language column in *The New York Times* to political correctness and offered up this definition:

> An adverbially premodified adjectival lexical unit used to attack liberal conformity on sexual, racial, environmental and other voguish issues.

And the conflict continued to grow into the next century. Sometimes academics unwittingly stepped into the fray. During a speech on January 14, 2005, Larry Summers, then president of Harvard, hypothesized that the shortage of women in certain disciplines could be explained by innate differences in mathematical ability. He was generously criticized in the media.

The excesses on both sides have resulted in vitriol and even silliness being slung between the political left and right. Charges of racism and complete insensitivity on one side, and of Marxism and killing the First Amendment on the other, have been hurled. Often, the debate has lost all semblance of courteous discourse.

"Offence is so easily given," wrote Lynne Truss in her book *Talk to the Hand*, published in 2005. "And where the 'minority' issue is involved, the rules seem to shift about: most of the time a person who is female/black/disabled/gay wants this *not* to be their defining characteristic; you are supposed to be blind to it. But then, on other occasions, you are supposed to observe special sensitivity, or show special respect."

Gad Saad, a social scientist and professor, contends that too much political correctness has produced an intolerable hypersensitivity:

> These politically correct language initiatives are misguided and harmful. They create highly entitled professional "victims" who expect to be free from any offense, and they engender a stifling atmosphere where all individuals walk on eggshells lest they might commit a linguistic capital crime.

But the war of words hasn't been without its lighter side. As early as 1992 at the Democratic convention in New York, a parody of the controversy was offered in the form of *The Official Politically Correct Dictionary*, which included replacing *ballot-box stuffing* with "nontraditional voting"; *cliché* with "previously enjoyed sound bite"; and *sore loser* with "equanimity-deprived individual with temporarily unmet career objectives."

Meanwhile, some real language changes were being instituted by the media and by the general population: "fireman" became "firefighter"; "policeman" and "lawman" became "police officer"; "mailman" became "postal worker"; and "mankind" became "humanity."

The business writer must be acutely aware of the political-correctness rules that exist in his workplace. But the best rule for finding the correct balance in all your business writing is to obey the basic tenets of etiquette: treat everyone with respect, consideration, and honesty.

A WORD ABOUT SNARK

Lewis Carroll's fanciful poem "The Hunting of the Snark" aside, what has become the intentionally meanspirited ridicule of individuals on the Internet and in the media, or "snark," masquerades as humor or satire. It is not. And it cannot be tolerated in the workplace.

Those who declare that beauty and class have long since gone out of business writing are right to condemn this kind of online discourse, which often makes the Internet seem like a classless and dangerous place. You can even see snark appearing in interoffice emails between colleagues.

The business writer must exercise extreme caution in whatever he posts or emails, because it is true that snark can make an immediately bad impression, and it never truly disappears.

Check yourself. Before you fire off a flip response or join in the "innocent" sport of "poking fun," take a few minutes to reflect. The Internet combination of anonymity, immediacy, and competitive one-upsmanship (or -upspersonship) can be enticingly dangerous. Stop before joining in online banter, and ask yourself: *Is what I'm about to dash off something I'd be happy to see on the front page of* The New York Times *as a quote from me?* Sure, that sounds dramatic, but what you post in private online can easily come back to bite you in a very public way, like during a job interview, a performance review, or a disciplinary-action meeting. There's lots of evidence that careers have been cut short because of what was intended to be a private online posting. As a business writer, you want all the things you post to come back speaking well of you, whenever and wherever you may meet them.

THE ISSUE OF LABELS

In the midst of what has often become overheated and distorted, it's important to remember that it's your job as a business writer to tread carefully within the bounds of using terms of reference acceptable to *all* those (or as many as possible) in your industry and organization. This takes both sensitivity and some serious detective work, because in one industry there may be no conventions against using terms of gender, like *draftsman, chairman, steward, stewardess,* or *councilman*; while in other industries, such terms are considered sexist. In many industries, terms that describe ethnicities must also be adjusted or eliminated.

We've seen the extremes of militant political correctness, where the use of a perfectly innocuous word spoken by a television and radio commentator will force the offender to profusely apologize or resign; in some cases, it will cause him to get fired. Accusations of political incorrectness can spread like wildfire over the Internet or be leveled in a nanosecond in the workplace. "Politically incorrect" isn't something you want as the main topic during your performance review. Nor do you want it listed on your permanent employee record as the reason you were dismissed.

So, try to write in a way that does not offend any reader on the basis of gender, race, ethnic origin, age, sexual preference, or disability.

To offer guidelines for avoiding offense, there have been many "bad word" tomes published, some by schools of journalism and major media sources. Check the most recent editions for your industry, but be aware that these sensitivities change, and then the terms change as well, and you will need to recheck them periodically.

GENDER TERMS: HE, SHE, THEY, OR YOU?

Writing with the acceptable gender reference may take a bit of maneuvering, too. Basically you have five choices:

1. Disregard any sensitivities on the matter and use the traditional approach of using the male pronouns, *he, him,* and *his,* in referring to all people: "Each employee may make *his* own choice." This works in some workplaces, but not all.

2. Use both genders in referring to all people: "Each employee may make *his/her* [or *his or her*] own choice." This approach can become tedious and can cause your readers to disengage.

3. Alternate between genders in your writing, sometimes using one, sometimes the other: "Each employee may make *her* own choice." If you use this approach, use the same gender throughout a short communication. You can help avoid confusion with this approach by inserting a parenthesis after the first "her": "(or his)." Or you can use an asterisk and, in a footnote, explain that "her refers to all employees, male or female." Then, in subsequent sentences, just use "her." This approach, most agree, shows both sensitivity and fairness.

4. Write using plural references: "Employees may make *their* own choices." This doesn't always work because it robs you of the personal and immediate tone you may be trying to achieve. Remember, too, you must be careful in using this approach that you have verb and predicate agreement. In this case, "choice" must be changed to "choices."

5. Sometimes you will want to change the sentence construction to avoid gender reference. You can achieve this by writing in the second person ("you"). "*You* may make *your* own choice."

Select the approach that's most acceptable in your industry and organization.

It's important to add that you may not always be able, as a business writer, to remain blameless in the game of political correctness. If the conflict becomes a choice between free speech and political correctness, err on the side of free speech. And let all your writing be guided by the principle of good business writing etiquette: treat everyone with consideration, respect, and honesty.

TIPS

- Be sensitive to everyone—colleagues, customers, clients, and the public—and address them as they prefer whenever possible.

- Respect everyone's right to self-describe. Privately asking a transsexual, for example, "What personal pronoun do you prefer?" is an approach that can eliminate a possible offense.

- Choose your words carefully. It's a difficult balancing act, but while endorsing the First Amendment and free speech you must also aim to avoid offending anyone.

- Use the gender term(s) agreed upon as acceptable within your industry and organization, or write around references to "he" or "she."

- Reach a consensus. Research your own industry and organization and decide with management the approach your organization will take. Then develop a list of all the acceptable and unacceptable terms. Once you have them, write a stylebook, or style sheet, to be used by everyone in the organization in writing to customers, colleagues, etc.; review and update it every six to twelve months.

- Don't use language that excludes, diminishes, or devalues any group.

- Don't use titles that are exclusionary, like *chairman, fireman, councilman, stewardess,* etc.

- Research and learn the currently acceptable words used for disabilities. Don't use words like "retarded" or "handicapped."

- Do not ask a colleague, client, customer, or applicant his/her age.

- Stay clear of asking about ethnic origins, religious affiliation, or sexual preference.

- Do not use religious terms in groups that may include people of different religions. For example, saying "God bless you" could be offensive to some.

- Don't ask personal questions that could be offensive, such as, "Do you have a boyfriend or a girlfriend?"

- Ask how colleagues and clients wish to be contacted. Make sure your communication habits and methods match the preferences of others: boomers undoubtedly prefer to be contacted by telephone, Gen Xers often prefer to communicate by email, and millennials prefer instant messaging and texting. Learn who prefers what and use these forms of contact.

- If you feel for ethical reasons you must freely express an opinion that may create an offense, know that there may be unpleasant consequences. Also, know that you can almost always express yourself without offending if you start from the motivation to show everyone respect.

PART THREE

THE SHAPES OF BUSINESS COMMUNICATIONS

The Email Animal (and All Its Electronic Relatives)

You've probably heard a colleague ask—or maybe you have asked—"How did we ever do business without email?"

Gone are the days of waiting for a reply by snail mail, hanging around the office after hours to get the letter you need delivered by FedEx, or lurking anxiously at the fax machine to get an official "hard copy." Often gone, too, is that frustrating game called telephone tag: you leave a message, making the messagee (receiver) "it"; then "it" calls you back and leaves you a message; and the two of you repeat this process a dizzying number of times before you actually talk to each other.

Email has utterly changed the workplace. It has sped up the rate of getting things done—like arranging meetings, immediately getting simple questions answered, or flipping a colleague something to review so you can instantly get his input.

It's important to say here that email has, in most offices, become synonymous with what used to be called a *memo*. Practically, emails are usually memos sent electronically, and they follow the memo form.

But in today's business-by-email world, you may hear much more about the dark side of email: the fact that each workday is filled with the frustration that there are two or more hours of valuable work time required just to wade through and respond to hundreds of emails. Many of them are totally unnecessary, some complete nonsense—the result of your colleagues' failure to properly think through the received question or request before firing off a responsive electronic missive that wastes your time and possibly many other people's time if it's posted on an email list where a number of people are participating.

Why is it, asks one executive, Bob, that email invites people to write without thinking? Why, indeed. Maybe it's the combination of the blank (void) that begs to be filled, that urgently blinking cursor, and the need the emailer has to feel productive. A lethal combination, as it turns out, in terms of producing email overload.

After spending over two hours untangling a snarl of email threads, another manager asks, "What produces these email cretins?" The answer, a third manager suggests, is that most people don't take the time to reflect on what they've written or to proofread it carefully before hitting SEND. The result is buckets of illiterate emails that are illogical, half-baked, wasteful, and sometimes even silly.

Email is anonymous, instant, intimate, and toneless. And it creates an artificial urgency for a response that perpetuates the process.

The typical business emailer, says Kevin, an IT executive, doesn't take the time to reread the communication he received to be sure he understands the message, is focused on the topic, and is offering valuable, new information in his response. Nor does he think through his reply, write an outline, or even jot down a few notes to use to organize his thoughts before his fingers begin to fly across the keys of his computer.

And no one, adds Sarah, a small-business owner, seems to bother to edit what he writes! Or make sure the spell-check has done its job.

Here's a too-typical case that illustrates the point: an IT manager at a leading financial institution, Jack, recently told me that he gets 150 business emails and electronic messages each day from subordinates and other managers in his organization. Each one requires a response *that day*. Many require an *immediate response*. He explained that this usually takes him over half of his workday, and he has to work between ten and twelve hours each day to try to get emails answered and to fulfill the real functions listed in his job description. The days he has to travel to corporate headquarters and branch offices for all-day meetings, he must sit up in his hotel room well into the early-morning hours to grapple with email.

So this chapter is aimed at helping Jack and you solve the problems presented by email; make emailing more effective; and increase everyone's productivity.

KNOW THE RULES

Recent research indicates that with so many modes of communication now available, it's necessary to factor in the preference of the participants in order to select the correct one. With these communication preferences in mind, the first rule to learn is a caution: just because you *can* doesn't mean you *should* email. It isn't appropriate for everything. Think about your message and your options. And remember, there are still some golden rules of etiquette and netiquette that need to be followed: (1) When a message is high in emotional content, it needs to be delivered in person, face-to-face; (2) When you need to express gratitude or appreciation, thanks, or sympathy, the proper vehicle must be a face-to-face meeting and/or a handwritten note that demonstrates the investment of time and care on your part.

FACE-TO-FACE

When what you have to say requires looking the person in the eye, your message needs to be delivered in person, face-to-face.

Personal. When your message is personal, use direct, face-to-face delivery because it's the surest way to be able to read body language and interpret visual and unspoken cues, voice inflection, and nuance. Personal messages require a human moment. (When disparate locations are involved, train yourself to effectively use Skype or another video vehicle for things like job interviews.)

Emotional. If you need to express thanks, sympathy, gratitude, or congratulations, it's best done in person, then followed up with a handwritten message that is (snail) mailed.

Negotiation. When the subject requires negotiation or extensive discussion, consider face-to-face as your first choice. It gives you the opportunity to immediately ask for an explanation, and it lets you interject and weigh in with your input, so you can more effectively and efficiently contribute and influence the outcome.

Personnel. Always conduct a job interview, a performance review, a firing, or an extraordinary request like asking for a raise or personal time off during a face-to-face encounter. (Use Skype or another video vehicle when geographic distance is a problem, but some training will be needed to allow you to obtain skills here.)

And remember: use a face-to-face meeting with others whenever that's what you would want someone to use with you.

TELEPHONE

Remember the telephone? For some colleagues (boomers, usually), the telephone is still the communication instrument of choice. It's also the best choice when you want to hear voice inflection and emotion; need to negotiate, especially if a matter has gotten tangled in a snarl of emails; need an immediate response; need the privacy a telephone conversation can afford (and you don't want to create a record); need to reach someone who doesn't use electronic devices routinely; want to discuss personal or personnel matters; or intend to send something you want to forewarn the other person about.

The biggest problem with the telephone is the fractured, unintelligible, and run-on voice messages that are left when the caller doesn't reach the person called.

So, before you telephone, jot down your main points. If you don't reach the person, leave a message by slowly and clearly giving your name and then a short, concise (slow and distinct) message that is to the point, as you've outlined in your jottings. At the end, clearly and slowly restate your name, your contact information (telephone numbers), and the best time and way to reach you. Repeat the telephone number.

LETTER ("HARD COPY" BY SNAIL MAIL)

Use a "hard copy" letter for official, legal documents (sometimes sent registered, recipient signature required); when an original signature is required or desired; when you want something official the recipient can reread and file, or treasure; or when there is highly confidential or complex content.

Use the letter for official business like a job acceptance, termination (after the face-to-face meeting), appreciation, recommendation, and employment contract.

Use a handwritten personal note for messages with social and emotional content (e.g., invitations, thanks, appreciation, sympathy, congratulations, and apology).

FAX

The fax has fallen out of favor since most organizations have enough capacity to receive large attachments by email. Still, faxing can be done directly from a hard copy or electronically by scanning and emailing. (A recent interview indicated that the pope still faxes.) Use the fax when you want a copy of a signature (usually legally binding), need to send hard letters or documents, or want the added security that what you send won't be intercepted by anyone other than your intended recipient.

EMAIL

Email communication has become a staple of the business world, primarily because it's immediate, allows users to disregard time zones, creates a permanent record, and allows responses to be posted whenever it's convenient. Email advantages include:

Exchange of essential information. When notices need to go out to a few or many, simple questions need to be asked and answered, or changes must be made, email works well.

Time to craft a response. You have time to consider and form a response.

Attach and include additional information. The recipient may print out attachments if and when he desires.

Informal discussions. Simple ideas and proposals may be easily and quickly discussed by email when two people or groups of people are included. The caution here is to be sure that you have guidelines and rules in place about posting and that someone monitors the "threads" so they don't become unwieldy or "forked" (a participant jumps in late, disregards the entire thread, and responds to just one early post, diverting the entire discussion).

Create a searchable record. When it's important to have a complete record, email can provide it.

Alter and edit copy. A working document, or manuscript, can be instantly passed from one person to another for editing, comment, and altering.

The bad news is that some of email's strengths are also its weaknesses. Here are some of the inherent problems:

Faceless and toneless. This often leads to misinterpretation and misunderstanding.

Unnecessary posting. The ease of emailing encourages unnecessary posting. Emails are often sent before the sender has given enough thought to what he intends to post.

Inappropriate emailing. Because it is easy to learn organizational email formulas, almost anyone can be contacted by email. This intimate characteristic of email has done away with the protective hierarchy, which used to be sacrosanct in most organizations, and it makes screening messages very difficult. The questions for many executives are: Should I allow support staff to manage my email? How many email addresses do I need? To whom should I give my "private" email address?

Interruptions. Emails can be intrusive if you interrupt your focus, concentration, and productivity when you stop working to open them and then respond. Research shows such interruptions and switching tasks take a decided toll on productivity. So schedule email and electronic response times (twice a day is enough for most people), and don't be tempted to wander into email at other times.

Searchable email record. Searchable records are good, right? But they can also come back to bite you: uncharitable colleagues or even courts of law can use them. Keep that in mind when you write. Never email something you wouldn't want to see in print in a very public place.

Forwarding. Whether by accident or intent, it's very easy for someone to forward your message to a recipient you didn't intend. Yes, your message is your creative work and should enjoy the protection of copyright, but that doesn't always deter people.

Edit. The ability to edit what is written is a good thing, but it also means that what you write can be edited and resent by others. For important or sensitive documents, use another vehicle to transmit material or attach what you've written as a PDF or other file that isn't easy to change. (We aren't talking about the use of Track Changes, where a number of people agree to work on a document or manuscript and are authorized to make changes—

this is often done between authors and editors of books, for example. And it can be both effective and efficient.)

Attachments. It's vital that you have a virus-protection system in place, because attachments can infect your computer system. Note that storage capacity can become a problem in some organizations not geared for large volumes of large attachments.

TEXTING (ON ELECTRONIC HANDHELD DEVICES)

While it's often the communication method of choice for millennials, texting for business should be limited to simple, very short, informal, and critical messages between two or a few people, when instant information needs to be transmitted, like out-of-the-office and on-the-go updates and confirmation of or changes to plans at the last minute. Use texting when you need to send a photo or keep abreast by instant mobile, silent, and surreptitious means. Don't overuse it, and don't abuse it. It interrupts the receiver.

Texts may be kept by individuals or on organization servers.

INSTANT MESSAGING (IM)

For team members working on the same projects, instant messaging can be a very effective way to get vital and timely information. But it can also be very disruptive. It works best with a small number of participants, and needs some strict rules to be effective. It can easily lapse into cross-messaging, and answers can get separated from questions. If some participants weigh in on only the last message, or the first after the discussion has moved on, things can get tangled, frayed, forked, and fractured. IMs are not easy for many users to recover after their computers have been shut down, so if you want a permanent record, use email or text.

WRITING THE EFFECTIVE EMAIL

To work best, your email needs to be *brief, focused,* and *complete.* Email writing is informal, but don't let that lull you into thinking anything goes. It demands the best skills of business-memo and letter writing—because it's now both. In her book *Sin and Syntax,* Constance Hale says, "Writing in a natural conversational voice takes some serious work." And the exact tone of informality can be very difficult to achieve. It must be appropriate to the person to whom you are writing, to the message, and to your relationship with the recipient(s). (The last is the trickiest. Sending an email that has an overly familiar tone to a colleague you don't know, or your boss, won't enhance your reputation.)

Don't casually shoot off an email before you've carefully honed your skills. What you write and send in haste you may regret for a very long time. So, to make sure your email measures up, run it through a few basic tests:

Purpose. Why are you writing? Do you have your purpose clearly in mind? The rule here should be one email for one topic. This facilitates accomplishing the purpose, filing, and making sure each email is complete. It also saves confusion when receiving responses.

Know your reader. Know who your reader is and what he knows about the subject. That will help you write a relevant message. Take a moment to think about your message from your reader's point of view.

As noted, your relationship to him is important, too, for deciding on the tone of your message. Make sure it's appropriate.

Add value. One of the biggest complaints in the workplace today is that many emails are completely unnecessary. If there's something you should know, or if you have a question you can answer yourself by reviewing emails without interrupting someone, do it. Don't add more email fodder to an already overloaded inbox.

Organize. Think through your message; jot down a few notes or write an outline; and complete any necessary research to make sure your message has real meat and potatoes.

Tone. Here's that word again, but it can't be overemphasized, since it portrays the attitude of the writer and how he regards both the message and the recipient. If you are writing to a colleague with whom you work closely and you have a friendly relationship, your message about obtaining a new client might begin, "Way to go! We nailed it in that presentation. They not only are going to sign with us, we'll have the contract tomorrow. And then it's champagne at 5:00 p.m."

To your boss, the email might begin, "This morning Jim Brent and I made the presentation to Baxter and Baxter's Sarah Jameston, CEO, and James Orbit, COO. They were very pleased with our proposal terms as outlined and indicated that they will execute the contract as written and deliver a signed copy tomorrow."

In a report to a wide audience and/or to the board of directors after the contract is signed and delivered, the text might start, "Baxter and Baxter are Signature's newest client, signing a contract for $4 million for our representation for . . ."

Draft. This is often best done first offline in a file, or at least before you type in the TO (address) line, so you avoid the possibility of prematurely blasting off a missive. This is the time to get your whole message down.

Edit. Know that your message will undoubtedly benefit from being cut by half. So trim it down. This is the time to rearrange anything out of sequence, lop off extra words (look for those extra -*ly* words), eliminate duplicate or superfluous information, and generally tidy up.

If the message is long by necessity, insert subheads, make them **boldface,** and use bullets. If you can indent, bring in the margins and double-space for ease of reading.

Make sure that your message has the right tone and that sentences and paragraphs are short. The best sentence length is fifteen to twenty words. (This isn't a strict rule, and depends on the subject. But if you have a string of thirty-five-word sentences, restructure them.) Vary sentence lengths for interest.

Proofread. Although you use a spell-checker, make sure you've used the right words. Read your message out loud for a final test. You may be surprised at what you find to correct. For a very important message, ask a couple of experts on the topic to read it and comment. This may give you vital feedback that will ensure your message is completely on target.

USE A POWERFUL SUBJECT LINE

Check your organization's rules here and comply. This can be the most important thing you write. Study newspaper headlines to see how to capture the essence of your email's content and express it in concise, precise, and compelling words—the fewer the better. Here's one from today's *New York Times*: "Arab Nations Strike in Libya, Surprising U.S." Use complete information that makes properly filing the email easy to do. For example, "Board Meeting," isn't enough information. You need "Board Meeting, April 23, 2015, Agenda," so everyone scanning their inbox knows exactly what it is and can decide when they should open it.

Some organizations use "ACTION" as a first word in the subject line to indicate a response is needed and/or an assignment is included. (Some organizations require that only those recipient(s) with "ACTION" in their subject line are allowed to respond. Everyone else is receiving the email for information only.) The overuse of "URGENT" has caused many organizations to restrict its use or prohibit it. Since ALL CAPS is the equivalent of shouting online, some organizations prohibit the use. Capitalize all major words except articles, prepositions, and conjunctions with fewer than five letters (unless they are first or last).

Practice coming up with effective subject lines, and try to keep the length to between five and seven words.

Don't continue to email on a thread when the subject has changed or forked until the subject line no longer reflects the content.

DECIDE ON THE SALUTATION

Because of the informality of email, the formal-letter salutation of "Dear Mr. Martin," when you are addressing a colleague, isn't normally used. Take your cue from your colleagues here or follow organization policy, if there is one. Usually the best approach is to use an informal greeting, but not an overly familiar one. "Hello Jim Brown," for a colleague you only know by name, or "Hi Dave," for a member of your team, works well. Some organizations do not use any greetings, and if you are emailing a group in a collaborative email thread, this is usually the practice.

USE AN EFFECTIVE SIGNATURE BLOCK

Making sure colleagues know who you are and how to contact you is vital. Most organizations use email "formulas" that make it easy for colleagues to contact you by email. But it's also useful (and sometimes an organizational requirement) that you use a standard signature block that lists your complete name, title, organization name, address (Web and physical address), and telephone number(s). If you develop your own email address, use your name. For outside communications, a signature may be part of the signature block. These can be set up so they appear automatically.

MAKE TO, CC, REPLY ALL, AND BCC WORK

Fill in the recipient TO field as the very last step in writing your email. This avoids premature send-offs. In some organizations, or on some teams, there are rigid rules about the use of these designations. One IT team, for example, requires that only the TO recipients may reply or weigh in. All the CC participants are on the list for information only. Know and carefully observe all such organizational rules.

A word about the lists of TOs and CCs: create a group address when a number of colleagues are on a committee or team or in a department to avoid huge listings before the reader ever gets to the content. And if you find yourself listed in a group inappropriately, ask to be removed.

REPLY ALL must be used with extreme caution. Be sure you know what your organization's policy is. Always double-check before hitting SEND, to make sure that you are not firing off a message to an unintended person. This has caused serious problems for senders. The other caution here is to be sure that in sending a personal message to someone, you are not attaching another email thread.

The BCC should rarely, if ever, be used. In many business cultures, it is regarded as overly political and even subversive. Check your organization's policy on this, but, regardless of the policy, take great care not to brand yourself as the office snitch.

A MATTER OF NETIQUETTE

Always exercise good netiquette. If your organization doesn't have a set of rules, review those at the end of this chapter and write up a set of your own. This will increase productivity and improve employee relations and job satisfaction.

There is never a reason to fire off a "flaming" email. If you are angry or emotional, give yourself time to cool down and regain composure. Because emails are faceless and toneless, offense is easily given. And taken. Don't be baited and respond in haste if someone fires at you. When emotions get elevated, it's time to call a face-to-face meeting and resolve things. If employees are located at different addresses, at least have a video- or telephone-conference meeting to get things back on track.

COLLABORATION

Collaborative groups or teams require special rules in order to make sure everyone is as productive as possible. Put strict rules in place, and insist people follow them.

COPYRIGHT/PLAGIARISM

Always follow the rule of copyright that states that whatever an individual writes is his unique creation and should not be quoted at length without express permission. Don't use anyone's written work without first getting their OK. Yes, there is a "fair use" rule that may apply, but in the workplace, it's best to ask. And when you do use someone's work, be sure to give full source and author credit. Not following this rule can amount to plagiarism.

It's important to note, too, that if your organization owns the electronic equipment and software you use, and perhaps even your work product, management can usually legally monitor all your electronic product, including your emails. Bear that in mind in writing personal emails at work.

TONE

It's fair to say that you will be known by the quality of your emails (to your colleagues, boss, clients, and customers). Writing great emails can be your ticket to the corner office.

TIPS

- **Establish email rules.** An organization-wide policy should be in place, and every employee needs to study and know the rules. The best way to get employee compliance is to involve as many key employees as possible in drafting the policy. Below are some sample rules you should consider.

Rule 1: *Only email content that you would be proud to have posted in a public place.*

Rule 2: *Represent the organization well* by employing proper netiquette: use standard upper- and lowercase letters; use proper grammar, punctuation, and spelling; follow organization email hierarchy in sending emails; edit and proofread all emails before sending; compress attachments according to organization policy.

Rule 3: *Personal emailing rules* should include if and when personal emails may be sent; if the organization reads personal emails and what is considered off-limits; if personal emails must be saved in a special folder; and whether employees may send or receive attachments—and, if so, which are acceptable. Personal email rules should also include any prohibited-content rules, such as creating and distributing offensive emails, including discriminatory content.

If the organization monitors employees' emails, this policy must be stated, noting that employees should not expect privacy for anything they write, store, send, or receive on the organization's computer system. Also state if the organization adds a disclaimer to employees' emails, and state the disclaimer text.

Rule 4: *Archiving emails* is required in many industries. Be sure all employees know and follow these rules. If archiving isn't required, let employees know the organization's policy on deleting emails.

Rule 5: *Confidential data rules and guidelines* should be known by all employees so proprietary information isn't disseminated.

Rule 6: *Email violations reporting and disciplinary action* policies must be clearly stated so employees know that breaching the rules will result in disciplinary action, up to and including termination. Also, state that employees are obliged to report abuses immediately, with full information. Be sure to appoint a person to whom infractions should be reported and specify the information to be included.

SAMPLE OFFICE EMAIL ETIQUETTE POLICY

Here's a sample set of rules that can limit nonsense emails and increase employees' productivity:

- Use FYI (for your information) and NRN (no response needed) whenever possible to eliminate unnecessary email responses.
- Only the employee(s) designated TO should respond to an email, and only if he/they have new and valuable information. All others copied should honor FYI and NRN.
- Do not email "me-too" messages to group email lists or routine thank-yous, statements of agreement, or messages to individuals within the group. Take all personal and person-to-person messages off-list.
- Do not use REPLY ALL unless the message is essential to everyone on the list.
- Update subject lines, and/or cut off threads when email discussions have frayed, or forked to another subject.
- Be sure to read a complete thread before responding to avoid derailing a discussion.
- Eliminate snarled email threads by telephoning or having a face-to-face conversation with a colleague when an email thread has become too complicated, confused, or emotional.
- Restrict email usage outside regular business hours (8:00 a.m. to 6:00 p.m., Monday through Friday).
- Use a group-calendar-based meeting scheduler for arranging meetings; don't use email.

- Limit email attachment size to 1MB unless you obtain the recipient's prior permission.
- Do not forward jokes or participate in rumors or gossip.

VACATION EMAIL PRACTICE

Make sure your vacation is free of email stress (or as nearly free as possible).

Step 1: Create an email address you give only to one colleague, or a very few with whom you must be in contact. (Tell him/them, of course, not to give the address to anyone.)

Step 2: Let colleagues and clients, friends and relatives know you will be out of contact, and when, and give them a contact person if there is something that can't wait. (This information can easily be put on your automatic email response, too.)

Step 3: Turn off and tune out. Being completely off the electronic grid recharges your brain. Make a habit of taking regular electronic-connection breaks—disconnect. Try regular meditation, daydreaming, or scheduled creative-time breaks to help retrain your impulse to electronically connect. You'll be amazed at the new crop of productive thinking this approach produces.

13

Memos That Make the Point

The memo form uses a prescribed list at the beginning:

TO:
FROM:
DATE:
SUBJECT:
cc:
bcc:

Some would say the memo morphed into email. Both use a structured format for ease of comprehension, and both usually have an informal tone. But, technically, email is the electronic messaging system that can carry many different kinds of communications—letters, reports, memos, minutes, proposals, etc.

Memos can either be sent as printed, paper documents or be emailed. And now in most business settings, the old nomenclature of "memo" doesn't exist. It's just called "email." But there are a few industries that still use the printed memo for employees who do not have access to organization email, such as production workers or some service employees—though this use is becoming rare.

METHODS OF DEVELOPMENT

The structure of the memo should use one of the following, or a combination, to give the reader the most immediate and logical access to the content. Use your message and your knowledge of the reader to dictate the best method of development from these options:

- ▶ *Cause-and-effect relationship* is based on just that, and can start with either the cause or the effect. It can work well for marketing reports, laboratory-experiment reports, accident reports, and many other direct relationship matters.
- ▶ *Chronological order* follows the time order in which things occurred. It works well for such things as accident reports, laboratory experiments, client sales development, and many other communications where time is the driver.
- ▶ *Comparison* works when you have one thing related to another, like reporting on how your new product stacks up against a competitive one (or more).
- ▶ *Deduction* (general to specific) method of development is useful when you want to make a case for a particular product or course of action by referring to a general fact or set of circumstances and drawing specific conclusions. It is an effective tool for marketing and sales and has many other applications. Deduction is useful when a general need underscores the efficacy of a specific product or course of action.
- ▶ *Definition* uses explanatory prose to give the exact meaning or description of the nature, or scope, of something. It can be effectively used to define a new process or procedure.
- ▶ *Division and classification* works well for separating the whole into its component parts, or for placing parts, or groups of parts, into their proper categories.
- ▶ *Induction* (specific to general) is the process of inferring (proving) a general law or case from a specific or particular example. It works well in such cases as using specific test results, when you aim to "prove" general conclusions.
- ▶ *Order of importance* (decreasing or increasing) is particularly effective when you need to rank items.
- ▶ *Sequential* uses the order of a process or procedure. It's especially effective for use in instructions for completing a procedure.
- ▶ *Spatial* development is useful in describing the physical appearance of something in all its dimensions.

You will often use a combination of these methods to state your message most effectively. You might, for example, describe the reorganization of departments by describing first the general to specific functions (deduction), then new operations (division and classification), and finally the workflow (sequential) within each restructured department.

CHECK FOR COMPLETENESS

Used effectively, memos provide a clear record of decisions made and actions taken. They inform, delegate, instruct, announce, request, and transmit documents. It's very important that you write strong, clear, effective, memos to help you grow your reputation as a successful business writer. (Also read and follow the guidelines in chapter 12, "The Email Animal.")

After you've completed each memo, give it a little shelf time, take one last fresh read, and check to be sure you've answered all these questions:

► Have I written the memo with the reader in mind, considering what he knows about the topic?

► Did I answer the *who, what, why, where, when,* and *how much* of my message?

► Have I followed a development method so my points logically progress?

► Have I used subheads, bullets, and short sentences and paragraphs to make my memo easy to comprehend?

► Does my memo flow?

► Do my transitions carry the reader from one paragraph (or point) to the next?

► Have I effectively drawn conclusions, a summary, my opinions, and/or a call to action?

TIPS

Use the following specific tips to check your memos.

- **Make sure your memos meet these general requirements:**

  - Keep references to race and gender out of your writing, and if you have questions about any aspect of your memo that could have legal implications, have it reviewed by an attorney.

  - Make sure your tone is informal, clear, and concise. Be sure that what you write is objective and free of possible offense. Use measured words and avoid extremes. "Never" and "always" aren't good choices; nor is it wise to include accusations and unfavorable characterizations.

  - Be specific; don't generalize; and document what you write.

  - Keep copies of your memos in your personal file to document your work; and if your organization allows it, copy superiors.

  - If you state a problem, offer a solution, alternatives, or possible courses of action.

- **Meeting announcements**

  - State the objective.

  - Outline the plan of action.

  - Assign tasks to colleagues to ensure they come prepared to participate.

  - Be sure you've answered *who*, *what*, *when*, *where*, and *how much*.

- **Meeting agendas**

  - Write with an action bias.

  - Include all contributions that participants must be prepared to offer.

  - Be sure to include *who*, *what*, *when*, *how*, *why*, and *where*.

- **Progress reports**

  - Use descriptive action heads and subheads.
  - Use action words.
  - Be sure you are both concise and complete.
  - Summarize, conclude, and/or call for action.

- **Personnel- or organizational-change announcements**

  - Be sure key colleagues are involved before general announcements are made. Organizational changes, policy decisions, and new procedures work best if colleagues have been consulted, have had the opportunity to give input, have been involved in the decision, and have "bought in." This reduces the chance that employees will feel blindsided and left out of the process.
  - Discuss with the individual employee who is being promoted, reassigned, or transferred in a verbal, face-to-face meeting before a written, general announcement is made.
  - For personnel appointments, include a statement or two about the person's interests and hobbies.

- **Bad news memos**

  - Be sure colleagues hear it from you first (not in a rumor or from an outside source), and give the bad news in person first, if possible.
  - Whenever possible, or unless you know the information will be taken well, start with a positive statement.
  - Give it to them straight. And immediately relate the action steps being taken to correct the situation, or what the next action step will be.
  - Take responsibility for whatever errors or misjudgments you (or management) have made, but don't grovel.

- State the impact on the organization and its members.
- Ask for specific cooperation or state action steps.
- Commit to keep members informed, state when (if you can), and keep that commitment.

- **Policy and procedure changes**

  - Be specific, and give the *who, why, what, where, when,* and *how* of the changes.
  - Use comparison development to show how changes will differ from the current policy or procedure.
  - Make responding easy.
  - Use heads, subheads, bullets, and numbers to make your points clear.

- **Recommendations**

  - Start with the recommendations, and why they are needed or important.
  - State briefly the benefits.
  - Summarize, restate recommendations, use a call to action, and give the next step to be taken (when and by whom).

14

Letters That Hit the Mark

The business letter is still the best vehicle for a formal communication sent to someone outside your organization. It is also useful when something both formal and official needs to be sent to a colleague inside the organization. Legal and financial communications are usually sent in a business letter, as are other kinds of official documents like contracts, employment, reprimands, and terminations.

But formal and official does not mean stuffy or pompous. Your letter should be written in a simple, straightforward style that focuses on the reader and his knowledge of the subject and that properly and respectfully expresses the level of seriousness of the message. Make it clear and concise, and use a tone that matches your relationship with the reader and the message, and you will accomplish the goal.

The business letter can be very effective in today's world of business by email because it has a special impact when it appears on your organization's letterhead and arrives in hard copy. But it can also be sent by email.

LANGUAGE AND TONE

Writing with the correct level of formality is the key. Being too casual or too familiar (when you don't have a close relationship with the recipient and your message is of a legal or financial nature) will brand you as inappropriate and possibly obtuse—you will undoubtedly offend the recipient.

Compare the following three letters to an employee with whom the writer has no personal relationship.

Too Familiar

Hi Dan,

Unfortunately, your request for a raise has been denied. Sorry. Maybe next quarter.

Sincerely,

Jack Sprat

HR

Too Formal

Dear Mr. Star:

Your request for an increase in remuneration in the amount of $7,000 per year, dated September 15, 2014, and received by this department on September 20, 2014, has been carefully reviewed first by your immediate supervisor, Mr. Roberts, and then by this department. We have compared your requested increase with organization standards, factoring in your performance reviews for the past quarter and your term of employment with Magic; unfortunately, we have determined that the discrepancy between the two, as well as the status of your accumulative performance reviews and length of employment with the organization, renders us unable to authorize the increase at this time. (Consult the employee manual 23.4 for a full explanation of the applicable regulation.) You may be eligible for an incremental remuneration increase on January 15, 2015, after your next performance review. It is your prerogative to again request an increase at that time.

Sincerely,

Jack Sprat

HR

Appropriate Approach and Tone

Dear Dan Star:

You've set a great example in your department, reports your boss, Sam Roberts. He has high praise for your work ethic, attention to detail, and overall performance, and he has recommended you be given the pay increase you requested. As you may know, every request must be in line with our organization's pay-scale policy, and I'm sorry to say that your request exceeds what is allowed for an employee with only six months with the company. (See the employee manual, section 23.4.)

I know this is very disappointing, but I'd like to encourage you to keep up your outstanding performance and reapply for a raise after your next performance review, January 15, 2015.

Let's sit down for a discussion next week on Tuesday at 2:00 p.m. in my office. I have a few suggestions you may find helpful.

Best regards,

Jack Sprat

HR

These three examples point out the need to match your writing to the reader and the message.

But first it's important to say that the first communication with Dan Star should be face-to-face and verbal. He should be told personally that his raise request was denied, and he should have been given an opportunity to discuss it with his supervisor and Jack Sprat of HR. Don't neglect this vital step in communication etiquette.

After the verbal discussion, a formal letter should be written.

In the examples, the first is too casual or informal, and the approach is dismissive and completely lacking in goodwill. The insensitivity and brevity make the letter inappropriate and even insulting. In the second example, the message is too formal and stilted, and is needlessly complex and wordy, confusing, and irritating. And it also completely lacks consideration for Dan's point of view. The third message strikes a good balance. The writing is simple, the words are clear, and it gives Dan valuable and important information while expressing empathy and inviting him to discuss the matter further, if he wishes.

BE SINCERE

No matter what the message, you will want to extend goodwill to the recipient, and you will usually want to enlist his cooperation.

The most sincere message that will build goodwill comes from an interest in your recipient and a desire to help him. Start by focusing on his needs and what you can do to benefit him. In your opening sentence to a person requesting a new operation manual, you will first want to tell him you understand his request, or you don't because you need more information from him. Here are a couple of examples sent by email:

Lacking Goodwill

You didn't include the model number of your auto analyzer in your email, so I can't help you.

> Best,
> I. M. Toobrief

Sincere

Dear Karen Mope,

I'd be happy to immediately send you a PDF copy of the operation manual you requested and mail you a printed copy, but I'll need the model number of your auto analyzer (on the plate on the back) to make certain that I send the correct manual.

Please shoot me an email with the number, and I'll get right back to you.

> Sincerely,
> Grace Bott,
> Customer Service

Write from the recipient's point of view—focus on his need and state his benefit(s) in your letter. Read the following responses to a request for a refund from a dissatisfied customer.

Not Reader-Focused

We must have a copy of your sales receipt before a refund can be considered.

Yes, this gives the recipient needed information, but it is written from the writer's point of view and implies that the customer may not receive a refund.

Improved

Please submit your sales receipt so we can verify your purchase and the date and then process any refund you may have coming.

While the tone is improved and the focus has been switched by asking for the recipient to act, the letter is still writer-focused. Try the following recipient-focused approach in your writing.

Reader-Focused

Dear Rachel Boom:

To receive your refund promptly, please fax or mail a copy of your sales receipt, and we will immediately process your refund.

This communication is both concise and reader-focused. It starts with the reader's need, states the reader's benefit, and requests action from her. Notice the use of the word "your" instead of "we."

But don't carry it too far. Avoid that false and ingratiating tone often heard from telephone customer service representatives who are trying to appease a dissatisfied customer with rote messages that start with "I'm sorry you are having difficulty," "I apologize for any inconvenience," or "We take every complaint very seriously." Not only do these statements sound as insincere as they are, but in the exchange that follows it's usually apparent they are untrue.

What do you think is wrong with the following examples?

Overdone "You" Viewpoint

Dear Mr. Grimes:

You are certainly one of our most valued customers, and as such, your satisfaction is our number one concern. Your letter expressing dissatisfaction with the model X vacuum system is therefore being immediately evaluated, and you will hear from engineering the very first moment all the tests have been completed and the problem has been resolved.

Balanced Approach

Dear Mr. Grimes:

Your problem with the model X vacuum system is being analyzed by engineering, and you will be getting a call from Robert Thomas, head engineer, by the end of the day. (You may call Robert at 000-0000.)

We understand the critical nature of your request and will work to fix this problem promptly.

Don't you think Mr. Grimes would be much more assured by the second letter?

Resist the temptation to write a letter that attempts humor at the recipient's expense or that is demanding, arrogant, overly authoritative, sarcastic, or negative. Instead, cool down until you can regain your reader-focused approach and use positive, tactful, respectful, and polite language.

GOOD NEWS

Use the direct approach when delivering good news—present it first in almost all letters.

Here's an example of a letter to a job applicant telling him he has been hired (after he was given the news verbally):

Dear Dirk Raider:

We are delighted to offer you the position of COO with Miracle Corporation. The entire senior management team, Susan Vader, Sam Nader, Rose Mader, and I, are all very enthusiastic about what you bring to our team. We know you will be a great asset.

The employment contract is attached. Please complete it and bring it when you come on Monday, and we'll complete all the employment busywork then.

Welcome to the Magic team!

Best regards,

Myrtle Chance

BAD NEWS

When what you have to say will be considered bad news by the recipient, your first job is to gain your reader's perspective and then decide how best to deliver your message. The best approach is usually *indirect*. First make a neutral or orienting statement that puts the bad news in as favorable or objective a context as possible, or one that shows empathy with your reader, so you may reduce the negative effect of your message. The next step is to explain the news; then deliver the news; and finally offer a positive closing.

The exception to this approach is if you know the reader well, and know he'll want to "hear it straight." Whichever approach you select, consider these points:

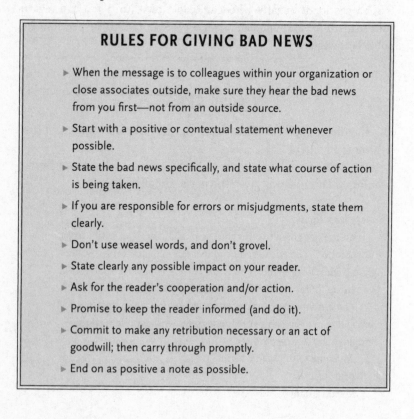

RULES FOR GIVING BAD NEWS

- ▶ When the message is to colleagues within your organization or close associates outside, make sure they hear the bad news from you first—not from an outside source.

- ▶ Start with a positive or contextual statement whenever possible.

- ▶ State the bad news specifically, and state what course of action is being taken.

- ▶ If you are responsible for errors or misjudgments, state them clearly.

- ▶ Don't use weasel words, and don't grovel.

- ▶ State clearly any possible impact on your reader.

- ▶ Ask for the reader's cooperation and/or action.

- ▶ Promise to keep the reader informed (and do it).

- ▶ Commit to make any retribution necessary or an act of goodwill; then carry through promptly.

- ▶ End on as positive a note as possible.

Here's an example of a letter that tells a friend and outside business associate that the writer's organization must withdraw sponsorship for a golf tournament because his organization has suffered an extreme financial loss. This news is best delivered face-to-face first, or at least by telephone. After that, follow up with a letter.

Dear Rick,

This year's golf tournament, it appears, will outpace last year's by a huge margin. Congratulations. It looks like a fantastic event, which makes my job even harder: I must tell you we will be unable to be a sponsor this year, due to the loss of a major client, Crescent Associates. It came out of the blue, and we will need to scramble to replace that organization in our client lineup.

We will miss our participation in your excellent event—I was hoping to win this year.

We look forward to renewing our sponsorship next year after we recover and get things back on track.

Best,

Jim

STRUCTURE

Think of your letter, which will appear on your organization's letterhead, in its component parts: (1) date; (2) inside address; (3) salutation; (4) opening or introduction; (5) body; (6) summary or conclusion; (7) complimentary closing; (8) signature; (9) signature block (when appropriate); and (10) end notations (when appropriate). You'll find this makes writing it much easier.

The completed letter should follow a standard format, and your organization may have selected one, so you will want to comply with that. The first printed format is the full block style, and the second is the modified block style.

In the full block style, all the lines start at the left margin, as shown on page 166.

Compass Management Group
1212 Broadway
New York, NY 00000

December 3, 2014

Mr. Chase Raines
CEO
Wired Well, Inc.
2020 Shattuck Ave.
Berkeley, CA 00000

Dear Mr. Raines:

Here is the market report with a complete breakdown of the plan we presented on Friday.

We believe Compass can help you achieve an increased market share for Wired Well using the approach we discussed, and we are eager to enter into a contract with you and begin this exciting program.

We're available to discuss any alterations to the plan you may desire and concerns you may still have, and I will contact you early next week to arrange a time.

We look forward to working with you to help make Wired Well an industry leader.

Best wishes,

Aubree Sidler
Project Manager

AS/bc
Enclosure: Marketing Report
cc: Forest Rangler

In the modified block style, the return address, date, and complimentary closing start at the center of the page. Here's how the same letter would appear in modified block style:

Compass Management Group
1212 Broadway
New York, NY 00000

December 3, 2014

Mr. Chase Raines
CEO
Wired Well, Inc.
2020 Shattuck Ave.
Berkeley, CA 00000

Dear Mr. Raines:
Here is the market report with a complete breakdown of the plan we presented on Friday.

We believe Compass can help you achieve an increased market share for Wired Well using the approach we discussed, and we are eager to enter into a contract with you and begin this exciting program.

We're available to discuss any alterations to the plan you may desire and concerns you may still have, and I will contact you early next week to arrange a time.

We look forward to working with you to help make Wired Well an industry standard.

Best wishes,

Aubree Sidler
Project Manager

AS/bc
Enclosure: Marketing Report
cc: Forest Ranger

THE ENVELOPE

Always put a return address on the envelope so your letter will be returned if it can't be delivered. And don't use a logo or design that messes with the placement of the return address or the addressee. I have had the postal service return letters in which the envelope bears a return address midway down the left side.

LETTER FORMAT AND FORM

INSIDE ADDRESS

Roy Peter Clark, in *Writing Tools*, relates the story of his editors and writing coaches at the former *St. Petersburg Times*, who always told reporters to not return to the office with a story until they had gotten "the name of the dog." A seasoned reporter recently told me that at the beginning of every interview he asks the person he's interviewing to print clearly his/her name. Why? Because it's the little details—and when you write a letter, the person whose name you misspell won't consider the misspelling of his name a "little detail"—that can derail your letter before you even get to the salutation. More to the point, getting the person's name, title, or organization wrong doesn't say good things about you and your attention to detail. Always double-check the name, title, organization, and address. If the gender is in question, check that, too. And when still in doubt, call the organization and find out.

SALUTATION

For someone you don't know, use the traditional Mr., Mrs., Miss, or Ms. and the last name. Or, for a bit of informality, if your message is informal, you may use "Dear John Doe." But don't err on the side of being overly familiar; you could give offense. If you haven't met Brooke Stoddard, don't address her (or is it him?) "Dear Brooke." If you aren't on a first-name basis, don't use only the first name in the salutation.

Doctors, judges, senators, professors, and other professionals worked hard to earn those designations, so use them. It's a sign of both respect and a certain formality and will always be appreciated.

An exception here is when you are writing to the director of marketing and don't know (and can't find out) the person's name. Address the positon: "Dear Director of Marketing."

SUBJECT LINE

In an overburdened business world, this line can save everyone time and can be very helpful in filing the letter correctly. This line may be indented or start at the left margin, and often begins "Subject:" or "Reference:" followed by a concise topic:

> Subject: Legal Action CA-945
> Reference: Legal Action CA-945

Sometimes the words are abbreviated as "SUB" or "REF," and sometimes only the topic is used. Both all-uppercase letters or initial capitals may be used.

BODY

The first sentence should clearly state the purpose of your letter. Try for writing that is clear; direct; specific, and to the point; complete; and concise. Follow that sentence with the details of your message, and be sure to include the *what, why, how, where, when,* and *who* so your recipient can take the action you desire.

CLOSING PARAGRAPH
SUMMARY, CONCLUSION, AND CALL TO ACTION

Some people have trouble saying good-bye. And some writers have trouble concluding their letters without lapsing into frivolity, filler, fodder, small talk, or stilted blather. Don't wax on; simply summarize, conclude, or make your call for action in your closing paragraph. Sentences like:

- It has been a pleasure serving you.
- Please contact us with any additional requests or concerns.
- Your speedy response in this matter will be greatly appreciated.

are OK, but they can be stated more simply or can be eliminated. Try:

- Thank you.
- We would appreciate your speedy response.

Be clear about the next step. If you are calling for action, state *who, what, when, where, why,* and *how.* Don't leave any doubt.

- Please return the contract by August 15.
- Please initial the changes on pages 4, 15, and 17 where marked; sign on page 24; then FedEx the contract back by Friday in the envelope provided.

Don't leave the reader wondering. And if you can, tell the reader what your next action will be and when:

- I'll call Thursday afternoon.
- I'll check with you tomorrow morning.

SIGNATURE

Make sure your sign-off, or complimentary closing, matches the letter content and your relationship with the recipient. Writers often select a complimentary closing and use it for all their letters, but "Best regards" or "Yours truly" is inappropriate for a collection letter, and "Warmest regards" and "All best wishes" don't work for a cover letter for legal action. Choose one of the following that fits best:

Sincerely,

Sincerely yours,

Best wishes,

Respectfully,

Respectfully yours,

Cordially,

Yours,

Yours respectfully,

Yours sincerely,

Yours truly,

All best wishes,

All the best,

Regards,

Best regards,

With kindest personal regards,

Or you may create your own. A friend always closes with "Cheers," which seems to work well for most letters.

WRITER'S SIGNATURE BLOCK

Your full business name is typed four lines below the complimentary closing, leaving this space for your signature. On the next line, under your typed name, type your title if it's appropriate. Under your title, you may wish to add your contact information, like a telephone number and email address, if they don't appear on the letterhead.

After proofreading your printed letter, sign your name beneath the complimentary closing.

END NOTATIONS

The traditional business-letter form uses the initials of the letter writer (who dictated the letter) in capital letters, followed by a forward slant, then the initials of the person who typed it in lowercase letters. (Sometimes a colon is used instead of the slant.) This is placed at the left margin, four spaces below the signature block for a short letter, two spaces below for a long letter. When you are both writer and typist, no initials are used.

If there are attachments or enclosures, these should be mentioned in the body of the letter, but also indicated below the signature block. And if you are sending a copy of the letter to another person, indicate that with a "cc:" followed by the person's name. When you wish to send a copy to another person but do not want the recipient to know you are doing so, you will note "bcc:" followed by the person's name on *your file copy only*.

ADDITIONAL PAGES

When your letter requires another page or more, carry at least two lines of the body of the letter to the next page. Second and following pages should be sent on the plain matching stationery without the letterhead. Type a header with the recipient's name, the page number, and the date either in the upper left-hand corner or across the top of the page.

TIPS

Use the following tips to make sure your letter is complete.

Acceptance Letter

- Focus on the reader, especially if you are accepting an invitation to a social event and are responding to the host, and start with your enthusiasm in accepting.
- Thank your reader for the invitation or offer.
- State your acceptance, expressing your pleasure.
- Confirm any details of the invitation or offer.
- End with a statement of anticipation.

Apology Letter (from the Offender) and Steps

- Remember that offending someone robs the person of power or diminishes him. Apologizing gives that power back.
- Write out your apology, even if you will give it verbally in a face-to-face meeting first. A written apology allows the reader to process the offense.
- Start by acknowledging the offense.
- State the offense and how you violated a moral code. (E.g., "Trix, yes, I did take the stamps from your desk drawer, then said I didn't. I should have asked you before getting into your desk or taking them. It was wrong of me. And I should have paid you back immediately.")
- Explain. Give any extenuating but relevant and valid information. (E.g., "I had to have the mailing out by the end of the day Friday and ran out of stamps at 5:45 p.m. I was scrambling to find fifty more stamps and remembered you kept a supply. Since you'd left the office, there was no opportunity to ask you. Then I rushed off to the post office to get the letters mailed and didn't return to the office. On Monday, I completely forgot about the stamps.")
- Communicate your regret. Here's the crux of the apology. Make sure you include a statement of your emotions of regret,

anxiety, and guilt. (E.g., "I understand that having someone rummaging in your desk and taking your supplies is a violation of your privacy. I felt terrible doing it, and I'm very sorry I did. I'm also sorry I didn't contact you Friday, own up, and tell you what happened.")

- Make reparations. An offense creates a debt that needs to be repaid. The apology itself is reparation, but you may also need to make the offended person whole again by repairing or replacing what was lost. (E.g., "I've left seventy-five stamps on your desk to replace those I took, plus extras.") Major offenses may require changes in behavior and restitution as part of the apology, particularly when the offense is of a legal nature.

- Offer an olive branch. To remove the residue of the offense, offer a positive act of friendship or cooperation. (E.g., "Several of us are meeting after work at Sam's for a drink. Would you like to join us?")

Apology Letter (Requesting an Apology)

- Take time to reflect and cool off if you're angry.

- Write how you feel to the offender, but don't accuse.

- Ask for an explanation. (E.g., "I value our working relationship, but I don't understand what happened. Please tell me.")

- When you have all the facts of the offense, ask for an apology. (E.g., "I feel you owe me an apology for going above my head in the office protocol.")

- Understand the reasons people won't apologize: pride; egocentricity; and/or fear of being rejected or being required to make amends.

- Whatever the outcome, treat the person honorably and respectfully.

Collection Letter

- State immediately that this is a collection letter.

- Ask the recipient to act.

- Put the responsibility to communicate or explain on the recipient, and make it as easy as possible for him to do.
- State the amount of the debt and the due date, and suggest a payment plan. Invite the reader to call and discuss it.
- Enclose a stamped, addressed envelope to make responding easy and/or include a telephone number.
- Try to work out payment terms in as flexible and generous a plan as possible.
- Use polite language and gradually use stronger language with each successive letter (if a number are required).

Complaint Letter

- Consider the best, most direct contact before using a letter. (If, for example, the neighbor's children are ruining your front lawn, first call and discuss the matter.)
- Cool down, if emotions are high.
- Research, gather information, and review all the facts, so you can put your complaint in logical, chronological order.
- Make notes and outline your complaint before you telephone or write.
- For social and personal problems, try to calmly and tactfully discuss them in a face-to-face conversation first. Use objective language (e.g., "To resolve this matter"), not personal language (e.g., "Frankly, I feel offended").
- Keep a complete record of dates and details, facts, persons, and contact information. This will allow you to be accurate and complete in your letter.
- Keep all your documents related to the issue.
- Write in a timely manner if a face-to-face discussion doesn't resolve the complaint.
- Begin with a positive fact. (If you are complaining about a defective product you've successfully used before, state your previous satisfaction.)

- Make one complaint per letter, unless there are a number of issues with one central problem.
- Give the complete facts in your letter, even if you have discussed it on the telephone or face-to-face.
- Address your complaint to a real person, not "customer service."
- State the problem in the first sentence and in the subject line.
- Use direct, specific language.
- Tell the reader why your complaint needs to be resolved, and how, in polite language.
- Use a third-party expert, if needed, to bolster your complaint.
- State a time frame for taking corrective action.
- Close on a positive and firm note, stating your confidence that the reader will resolve the complaint as you have outlined, and give a date when you will contact the reader again, if you feel uncertain he will respond favorably, or if you want to negotiate.
- Include copies of any documentation that proves your case, like photos.
- Give your complete contact information.

Condolence/Sympathy Letter

- Empathize with the distressed or bereaved person.
- Write as soon as you hear about the bereavement or loss, using your relationship with the recipient to guide what you write and your tone.
- Focus on the recipient, and don't misdirect your message to your feelings or let your focus stray into relating someone else's problem, etc.
- Open with a simple, strong message of sympathy, naming the loss or event for which you are writing. Avoid harsh words like "dead," "killed," "deceased," "bankrupt," "broke," "homeless," or the like. (Save long messages that reminisce about a loved one for later.)
- Be hopeful, and avoid tones of pity.
- Relate a brief, warm, fond memory of the deceased, if appropriate.

- Consider the religious preference, ethnic mores, family wishes, and organizational customs of the bereaved, and don't write anything that could be offensive.

- Include a message of sympathy to family members and associates, when appropriate.

- Make a specific offer of help and explain how you will follow up to carry through on your offer.

- Close on a warm note.

  In addition, you may wish to do the following:

- Ask the mortuary, in the case of a death, if the family has a request for tributes or contributions.

- If you send flowers, write a message to accompany them.

- Inquire of the mortuary, or a designated family member, what else would be helpful, if you wish to volunteer to do something additional to help.

Contract Letter

- Research thoroughly, and know your rights and obligations and those of the other party.

- Outline each party's duties, responsibilities, remuneration, benefits, and liabilities. (Consult relevant contracts and experts.)

- Anticipate what could interfere with the partnership's success and write "in the event" provisions into the contract.

- List all terms of agreement, such as supplies to be used, start date, finish date, inspections to be done, and approvals.

- Provide alternative sources for satisfactorily completing your agreement for both parties.

Cover Letter

- Address a recipient.

- Make it short and to the point: state what is enclosed, attached, or being sent under separate cover.

- List the number of enclosures or briefly list the contents, if appropriate.
- State the purpose of the contents and who authorized them.
- Explain how to use the contents, if appropriate.
- Include your complete contact information.
- Conclude with a goodwill statement, appreciation, and action to be taken.

Fund-raising Letter

- Start with an attention-getting sentence. (E.g., "Paloma Esqutar will go to bed hungry tonight.")
- Identify the charity and its purpose. (e.g., ". . . unless she receives a food package sent by Food for Kids").
- State how the reader can help. (E.g., "Your contribution of $50 will ensure Paloma and three other children will eat for a month.")
- State the benefits of the reader's contribution to the recipients.
- Explain the benefits of contributing to the reader, tuning your language to him. (E.g., "Helping children makes you feel good.")
- Use a tone and language that indicate you expect the reader to help.
- Make contributing as easy as possible. Enclose a postage-free, addressed envelope.
- Include a mission statement, telling the reader what you want to accomplish and where you are in meeting your goal.

Letter to the Editor

- Inquire to learn the policy of the publication and its editorial requirements about letters to the editor. (Requirements differ. Most publications allow five hundred to eight hundred words in a letter.)
- Weigh the facts that letters to the editor can produce: the potential for visibility and publicity, which can be both positive and negative.
- Be sure your management team is onboard with a decision to write

(get official approval), if you are writing something about the organization.

- Read many letters to the editor in the publication and check the approach and tone, then follow the requirements, specifications, and guidelines.
- Write with a positive approach in an upbeat tone.
- If you are writing in response to a letter to the editor that appeared in the publication, refer to the title, writer, and date. State your position and support it with data and facts, giving sources and authorities. Focus on a few points, and be clear, objective, and brief.
- To correct inaccuracies or mistakes in previous issues of the publication, refer to the date, page, title, and author. Cite the inaccuracy or mistake, then state the correct information, naming expert sources.
- Sign your letter with your name and, if applicable, title.

Negotiation Letter (and Discussions)

- Research and gather as many facts about the reader (negotiator) as possible. You'll want to know strengths, weaknesses, financial standing (if relevant), and past similar negotiations and outcomes.
- Determine how you may best approach your reader.
- Be willing to compromise.
- Create two lists for your own information: (1) the optimal outcome you'd like to achieve, and (2) the minimal outcome you'd accept.
- Ask the other negotiator(s) to do the same.
- Consider using a mutually agreed-upon arbitrator (third, independent party) to assist in the process.
- Listen to, or read, the other negotiator(s) list(s) and ask for any clarification you may need.
- Restate the terms to be sure you understand.

- Make a statement of goodwill that indicates you want to arrive at a mutually fair result.
- Brainstorm any other possible results with the other negotiator(s).
- Offer concessions and request concessions to move the process toward a satisfactory conclusion.
- Discuss areas of nonagreement, maintaining a spirit of give-and-take.
- Conclude the negotiations with a written list of agreed-upon terms.
- Give everyone time to reflect on the negotiated terms, if necessary, before entering into an agreement.

Pitch Letter

- Study and understand the subject or product until you can explain the noteworthy features well.
- Know the target market's potential interest in the subject or product.
- Find out the correct person to contact.
- Call the person (network your way to the person, if you can); if possible, make a verbal pitch, stating you will follow up with a written one.
- Ask the person's preferred way to receive your pitch—email, mail, or fax. (Offer an exclusive if this will allow you to get the feature coverage you want.)
- Be sure you have the correct spelling of the person's name, the title, and the address.
- Carefully craft your letter, slanting it to the audience.
- Use an intriguing "hook" in your first sentence and paragraph. It can be a news angle, a personality angle, or a need or desire of the target audience.
- Write with a friendly, informal, and professional tone.
- Make the pitch short—no more than a single page in length, being sure you've included the important information.

- Conclude by asking for the feature coverage and promising to make the next contact, and specify when. "I'll call you Wednesday to follow up."
- Follow up as promised.

Refusal Letter

- Write as promptly as possible, using an indirect approach, unless you know the recipient and know he will appreciate a direct approach.
- Start with an explanation. (E.g., "Thank you for your application.") Then walk the reader through your rationale for the refusal. (E.g., "We had over fifty applications, twenty-five of which had the exact experience we were seeking.")
- State a point of agreement or empathy with the recipient. (E.g., "We appreciate the fine work your organization, Boy Wonder, is doing.")
- Make your refusal clear, unequivocal, and positive.
- Be tactful, even if the request is unreasonable.
- Include a counterproposal, compromise, or suggestion, if possible. (E.g., "We will be happy to consider a donation next fiscal year.")
- Close with a goodwill statement. (E.g., "We wish you well with this year's program.")

Request Letter

- State immediately *what* you want.
- Tell the recipient who you are and why you want what you want.
- Express advance *thanks* for the recipient's cooperation.

Settlement Letter

- Review the details of the original agreement.
- Research all relevant laws; restrictions; facts about accepted current practice; financial debts, expenditures, and liabilities; infractions by the other party, etc.
- Consult an attorney and any other experts who may have pertinent information or knowledge.

- Make a full assessment of the situation.
- Allow a cooling-off period if emotions are elevated. (Relinquish any revenge motive and remove any inflammatory words from your discussions.)
- List in detail the points each party agrees to.
- Conclude by stating that this is the complete and final settlement agreement between the parties on the matter (and describe it precisely, including legal case numbers and any other defining details, so it will never be disputed or confused).
- Have the settlement letter reviewed by a trusted attorney who specializes in pertinent laws.
- Be sure both parties sign and date the settlement.
- File it, or have it notarized and filed with the proper entities.

15

The Business Plan
That Gets Action

The business plan requires your best *persuasive writing*. It must tell your story and end in a compelling call to action that motivates your audience to approve and fund your plan. Whether you describe a new project for your existing company or propose a start-up business, your plan must state your purpose and goals; outline your mission, objectives, strategy, and procedures; and get your audience to take the action you want.

START WITH THE AUDIENCE

The first step is to know the audience you are targeting. Do you want to convince managers in your organization to approve the development of a new product? Persuade a bank to make a loan and extend a line of credit? Or convince investors to fund your new business idea? These factors dramatically affect the approach and content of your plan.

Focus on your audience—and the *individuals* you're trying to persuade—before you start writing. Know what they want to see in a plan; then analyze what you need to provide in your plan to appeal to them.

Start with your organization's management team. To convince your team to approve a new product or business venture, first analyze each manager and the organization's approval criteria and process. If possible, and at each stage of development, discuss your idea with each manager to get his input and to garner his early cooperation and support. This will increase your chances for success. Managers will want to look at the potential market, future profitability, and the fit of the new product (or venture) with the organization's mission statement and goals.

Banks will want to see the financial history of the organization (if any), as well as a balance sheet, profit-and-loss statements, a three-year cash-flow projection (and sometimes projections, expenses, and the sources and use of funds statements). Ask your banker exactly what he wants included in your plan (or loan package) to save time and increase your chances of success.

KNOW YOUR PURPOSE

Once you understand your audience and know what will be convincing to them, pull together all the information you'll need and assign the writing of segments of the plan to the right experts.

WHAT TO INCLUDE

You will need to include some or all of the following information:

- ▶ Market analysis
- ▶ Key financials (e.g., profit-and-loss statements, sales projections, cash-flow analysis, expenditures, and/or balance sheets)
- ▶ Résumés of members of the management team
- ▶ Licenses
- ▶ Contracts
- ▶ Patents
- ▶ Favorable publicity
- ▶ Endorsements from experts
- ▶ Support statements from experts
- ▶ Ancillary outside support and services (banking relationships, attorneys, CPA or financial advisors, subcontractors, supply and manufacturing sources, etc.)
- ▶ Anything else that helps you make your case, like research or scientific papers that indicate there's a need for your product

Divide the plan segments into the respective parts others must do, and coordinate with them to get the segments completed.

The length of your business plan will be determined by the audience and the venture you are writing the plan for—but the shorter, the better. Typically, the basic plan will be anywhere from one to ten pages and will be bound together with tabbed appendixes of supplemental information for the items listed above.

You will undoubtedly be presenting your plan verbally, possibly using PowerPoint or another visual aid. And you'll be passing out copies of the plan for your audience to look at, review, and take with them for further study. Certainly the verbal presentation is key, and it must be done in simple, clear terms and with enthusiasm.

Think about ways to help carry your message, such as visual aids.

Here are the elements that you may want to include as segments of your basic plan:

- ▶ Title page
- ▶ Executive summary or business description
- ▶ Vision
- ▶ Mission statement
- ▶ Objectives
- ▶ Market analysis
- ▶ Marketing plan
- ▶ Strategies
- ▶ Financial analysis
- ▶ Action plan
- ▶ Appendixes and supporting documents

BRAINSTORM AND RESEARCH

Brainstorm with key managers, collect information, and outline your plan. Developing a successful plan usually requires receiving vital input from quite a few people.

Thoroughly research every aspect of your plan to be sure you have complete information. You don't want, for example, to find out after your presentation that you missed a competitor in the market space for which you are proposing a product.

At the same time, you must remember to keep the plan simple and straightforward, eliminating irrelevant and nonessential information. Be ready to answer questions on secondary issues and details at the end of your verbal presentation or in follow-up discussions.

START WRITING

First document the *need* or *desire* (market) for your product. This requires a complete and honest evaluation of the competition.

If you define the *need* correctly, you will be able to present your product as the *solution*. But your case must be made in logical and progressive yet concise steps.

Underestimate things like projected sales figures. It is much better to exceed projections than to fall short.

Decide which of the following segments you will include to tell your story. Then write and arrange those you need to build a persuasive plan, making each segment short and compelling.

Executive summary / business description. This is a concise, complete overview of the type of business, products, and services. If the business is in operation, present market position or share. Here, or on the title page, include the following items that apply:

- ▶ Business legal name and status
- ▶ Physical or virtual address
- ▶ Description of its operation—what it does
- ▶ Market information—present market share and growth potential
- ▶ Competitive position—unique features that will result in product sales over competitive products
- ▶ Future development—new products or services

Vision statement. This is the blue-sky segment, where you describe the future of the business—where it is projected to be in one, three, five, and perhaps ten years. Keep your statements rooted in the facts you present.

Mission statement. This is the heart of the business's purpose and reason for existing. Make this as simple as possible. For a bank's new customer-software program, for example, the mission statement could be, "Cash Now will eliminate overnight withdrawal errors."

Management team. Sometimes your key management-team members are so impressive that you will want to lead with this information and offer it as one of the primary reasons the business should be approved and funded. If that's the case, put it right up front and include the résumés in the appendixes. List each team member and give his individual expertise. Also list outside support-team members, like consultants, attorneys, accountants, insurance agents, marketing experts, manufacturing sources, and other experts with whom you've established a relationship and the commitment to work with the business.

Objectives/goals. This is where you'll state the specific, measurable goals of the business in well-defined, quantifiable, and measurable terms. Include both short-term and long-term goals. This builds accountability into your plan. Prioritize and edit your list to the most important items. The goals may be divided into financial, marketing, revenue, profit, manufacturing, operations, personnel, etc. This segment should include your business targets for specific time frames. Again, be conservative rather than overly optimistic. It's much better to look more successful than you estimated in six months or a year than to look as if you didn't project properly or you underachieved.

Strategies. Well-focused strategies are the operating procedures that will define your business and keep it operating on target. Address here both the inside market influences and the external influences that you will use to help your business grow.

Market analysis. This is the core of your plan. This segment must demonstrate that you understand the market and the competitors your business is up against. Describe how your business will be able to compete and become successful. List each competitor and analyze why and how it has secured its place in the market. Then describe how your product or service will vie with each competitor and win a profitable market share.

Marketing plan. Here is where you will describe in concrete terms when and how you will launch your business. List the kinds of advertising, public relations, networking, Internet blogs or postings, and other instruments you will use and include all the relevant details.

Financial analysis. This financial-plan segment is often the most difficult to develop. You must present the financial history and projections about financial growth. Again, don't sugarcoat the information. Present both financial strengths and weaknesses. Cash-flow projections and cost-control factors are critical. Be sure to include scenarios of problems that could arise and how you plan to prevent or overcome them. Use colored charts and graphs to help the audience visualize this information. (But don't go overboard here. Too much sizzle can dwarf your verbal message.) Draw a complete picture (full disclosure) of all the financial liabilities and debt the business has.

Action plan. You may elect to include a segment that lists specific actions that your business will take to achieve the objectives and goals you've listed. Specific tasks should have deadlines, and it's best to assign tasks to specific key managers or supporting associates. You will also want to include here estimated costs and a time frame for each of the tasks. You may also want to include alternate plans, e.g., if "A" and "B" happen, we will do "E" and "F."

Appendixes. All the supporting documents should be tabbed and arranged in the order referred to in the business plan, and bound behind it. This will include things like résumés, endorsements, bank letters of approval, statements from outside supporting experts and associates, publicity coverage, scientific papers and reports, competitive products or procedures, contracts, patents, and anything else that helps in telling the full and positive story for your product or service.

TIPS

- Be sure you can write in a single sentence what the purpose of your business is.

- Take your time in developing your business plan and get input from experts inside and outside your organization.

- Be sure to query the audience of your plan before you develop it to find out exactly what they want to see in a plan. Different audiences require different things.

- Make an in-depth study of the individuals to whom you'll be presenting your plan. This could be key to helping you develop a winning plan.

- Use your business plan as a tool for measuring the progress and success of the business, and update and alter it as the business develops to keep it current.

16

The Report That Changes Things

Reports are the lifeblood of every business. They inform those who need to know so that decisions can be made and business can move forward. Reports come in every stripe and size, from a paragraph or two to hundreds of pages. And they cover all kinds of functions from expense reports, aimed at getting reimbursed, to boards of directors meetings (minutes), aimed at recording decisions; from R & D reports, aimed at describing progress and directing new research, to annual reports, aimed at giving an account of the business's operation for the year.

The sole purpose of the business report is to communicate what has happened—or is happening—and possibly recommend what should be done next.

Writing reports well will mark you for success as a business writer.

The writing style, structure, and tone in reports range from the very informal to very formal.

Informal reports are usually completed in a conversational tone and cover short-term information. They usually appear in your email inbox as memos that disclose the monthly financial status, recent field activity, or things like weekly or monthly test results or the latest management decisions. Formal reports use a more formal tone and are more structured, often using an indirect style.

For either type of report, be sure to follow these steps:

1. *Analyze your audience.* Know to whom you're writing, and what they know about the subject.

2. *Know the facts.* Be a reporter and keep meticulous notes on every fact of your subject. If it's an incident or accident report, for example, take photos at the time to document facts, save any physical evidence, and record complete information of times, personnel involved, witnesses, and contact information. Write immediately, when the details are clearest.

3. *Start with a purpose.* Often the type of report gives the purpose—for example, "expense report" or "progress report"—but if not, make it clear in the first sentence: "The client meeting decisions made were: (1) start the ad campaign on October 1; and (2) simultaneously start the public relations plan."

4. *Use a solid structure.* Your organization may have a prescribed format. If so, use it. If not, make sure you've included a concise statement of the *facts or findings*; a *summary* (this sometimes comes at the beginning in an executive summary); a *conclusion*, which wraps up the meaning of the findings; and *recommendations* or *next actions* to be taken. Use subheads and bullets to help the reader quickly grasp the information.

5. *Be concise and thorough.* Returning frequently to your purpose statement will keep you on track in delivering all the essential elements of *what, who, when, where, why,* and *how.* Use objective, complete, and unbiased language in the body of your report. Opinions, interpretations, and recommendations need to come at the end and must be labeled as such. These are usually given under the conclusions or recommendations subheads. Don't color or inflate the facts to make a point, and don't leave out negative information—that needs to be reported, too.

REPORT FORMAT

Use labeled sections and subheads to guide your reader. Select sections consistent with your organization's protocol, as well as those that help you tell your story in the most readable, clear, and concise way.

FRONT MATERIAL

This is where you'll describe the report's purpose, give an overview, list contributors, and include a listing of specific content.

- ▶ The **title page**, the first page, gives the title and author(s). It sometimes also lists sponsoring persons or organizations, date of issuance or period, and the name of the commissioning organization. The page isn't numbered but counts as page i. (The back of the page, also unnumbered, is page ii.)
- ▶ **Letter of authorization**, when used, lists the sponsoring organization (or person) that commissioned the report. It is numbered with lowercase Roman numerals: iii.
- ▶ **Letter of transmittal** is a cover letter that identifies by whom the report is sent, and to whom it is being sent. It draws attention to certain sections and major points of the report.
- ▶ **Abstract** is a synopsis, or summary, of the major points of the report. This is usually limited to 200–250 words.
- ▶ The **table of contents** is a listing of heads and subheads in the report and the page numbers on which they begin.
- ▶ **List of figures** (when there are five or more) gives the figures and page numbers on which they appear.
- ▶ **List of tables** (when there are five or more) gives the tables and the page numbers on which they appear.
- ▶ **List of abbreviations and symbols** gives a quick index for all those used to give readers a quick reference.
- ▶ The **foreword** introduces the report. It's written by someone other than the author(s), giving background and sometimes comparisons with related reports. The foreword author's name and the date appear immediately at the end.
- ▶ The **preface**, when included, is the author's statement about the history, background, purpose, and scope of the report. Sometimes it includes recognition of people and organizations that provided assistance in funding and compiling the report.

BODY

This is the meat of your report. Use a logical progression that presents the most comprehensive and concise narrative. Include the methods, procedures, tests, and comparisons used, as well as the results, analyses, findings, conclusions, and recommendations or next steps to be taken. Select the sections consistent with your organization's protocol and the scope of your report. You won't use all of these.

> ▸ The **executive summary** is an overview of the highlights of the report. It shouldn't exceed 10 percent of the length of the report, and it should be aimed at decision makers.

> ▸ The **introduction** sets up the account that will follow by giving readers background knowledge that will help them understand the report. Be sure the complete subject, purpose, scope, and any pertinent explanations and approaches used and research are covered here.

> ▸ The **text** describes in detail how the study, investigation, tests, and research were done and gives the initial findings.

> ▸ The **conclusions** or **summary** distills the results, findings, and outcome, and offers the conclusions drawn.

> ▸ The **recommendations** section offers a course of action or lists possible courses of action based on the conclusions, and sometimes it gives the next step to be taken.

BACK MATERIAL

This is where you list sources, offer documentation, and provide other supplemental materials.

> ▸ **References** list studies, books, magazine articles, Web references, surveys, and interviews referred to in the report. A listing of the page numbers makes this most helpful to readers.

> ▸ The **bibliography** is a listing of the published sources and Web sources used in researching the report.

> ▸ The **glossary** is an alphabetical listing of terms and definitions used in the report.

> ▸ The **index** uses key terms, subjects, or names with the page numbers on which they appear, so readers can find specific information.

TYPES OF REPORTS

Specific types of reports take on a style that becomes familiar to readers and allows them to quickly find and understand the message. Here's a list of descriptive elements found in specific reports.

PROGRESS (ACTIVITY) REPORT

This report is written to provide decision makers with information on the status of a project, usually to keep them informed about scheduling and budget issues. It is prepared by subcontractors for contractors, contractors for a client organization, and project managers for supervisors. It's usually written on a regular timetable to avoid scheduling conflicts and cost overages. When done properly, it helps projects of all kinds run smoothly, by allowing managers to efficiently order supplies, schedule work, assign work, and adjust budgets as needed.

FEASIBILITY REPORT (RECOMMENDATION REPORT)

Organizations usually start with a perceived need, then develop this report to investigate whether new equipment, a new service, space expansion, or a change in operating procedures will have the desired successful result—cost savings, increased production, etc. Undertake a thorough investigation and conduct careful research to present all the facts and projections. Use objective reporting to produce this report and divide it into introduction, body (background, scope, comparisons), conclusion, and recommendations. This is not a proposal that is based on persuasive writing, but if you are convinced of the success here, your opinion should be included in the recommendations.

TRIP REPORT (REPAIR REPORT, SERVICE REPORT)

Used for field-service problems, maintenance, installation, or other business, this report documents what was accomplished and when. Organizations often have a specified format to follow and distribute the report as a memo, through email.

Usually sent to your immediate supervisor, it may also be sent to a number of managers to provide them with important information on results. Use the subject line to identify the customer, location, inclusive dates of the trip, and sometimes the purpose: "Miracle Landscapes, Roanoke, New Jersey, April 10–12, 2014. Repair."

Use your organization's prescribed format or divide the report into these sections: problem (or reason for the trip), action taken, conclusion, and sometimes recommendations. Make your report both thorough and concise. Often an expense report is attached, or cost information may be part of this report.

EXPENSE REPORT

This report is usually written by an employee to his supervisor and gives a simple sentence or two of explanation, listing expenses and attaching receipts. Most organizations have a prescribed format, which you must follow.

INVESTIGATIVE REPORT

This report is produced after a request for information initiates an inquiry about such things as competitive product pricing, competitive positioning, customer product satisfaction, a possible change in operation or procedures, etc.

Complete it in an informal tone in a memo, which can be transmitted by email.

Start with a brief statement of the purpose of the report. Then write an introductory summary stating the background or reason for the inquiry. Next, give the scope of your investigation and follow that with a concise statement of your findings and conclusions. Opinions and recommendations, if any, should be labeled as such and included at the end.

TROUBLE REPORT (ACCIDENT REPORT, INCIDENT REPORT)

Maintaining a safe work environment and documenting any accident or incident that could result in legal action or an insurance claim drive this report. The subject may be an equipment failure, an employee injury, negligence, or other kinds of health injuries. Make sure an objective and complete accounting of the facts and times is recorded, and include a complete record of witnesses and those offering assistance and aid, along with their contact information. This report is made for internal organization use. Be aware, however, that it may have a much wider distribution—if, for example, an employee injury results in an insurance claim or legal action.

The memo form is the usual format, unless your organization uses another specific form. The report will be sent to the supervisor or other organization-designated administrator. The subject line should include a concise description and the date and time, such as "Production Line Accident, Line B, May 15, 2014, 2:43 p.m."

You want to answer these questions: What happened? When did it happen? Where did it happen? Who saw it happen? What did they report? Was anyone injured? Was there damage to equipment? Was there work stoppage? Were outside experts called? If so, who, when, and what did they do? Was anyone taken to the hospital? If so, where and when?

Start the first sentence with a statement of the incident or accident; give a complete and concise account of what happened, with details; and end with conclusions and a list of witnesses and contact information. Some reports may end with actions to be taken or recommendations, too. But when personal injury is involved, be cautious about providing opinions. Often the best structure for the body of your report will be a recording of the precise time and what happened. Here's an example:

Mayberry Motors, Inc.
Accident Report

TO: James Boil,
           Director of Safety
FROM: Julie Grover,
           Line B Supervisor
DATE: May 15, 2015, 4:00 p.m.
SUBJECT: Production Line B Accident,
           May 15, 2015, 2:43 p.m.

Accident Summary

Alice Jitters, assembly line worker, was injured when she slipped on spilled water on the assembly line floor at her station. She fell against the conveyor belt, causing a gash to her right temple, and injured her hand when she hit the floor while still holding her power wrench.

Occurrence Details

1. Alice, who was not wearing her required safety shoes, slipped on water on the floor, which she had spilled moments earlier from a bottle she'd placed within the assembly area on the floor (a violation of rule #37).

2. Dedra Isaac, Alice's assembly partner, stated that Alice was stepping into position to tighten a bolt when her right foot slipped, and she fell against the conveyor belt, then to the floor. Dedra reported that Alice's right temple hit the conveyor belt, which produced the laceration.

3. Alice was conscious and talking when I approached her immediately after the accident, at 2:44 p.m., and she complained that she'd hurt her wrist when she hit the floor. I applied compression to the right temple laceration, which was about two inches in length, stabilized the wrist, and called emergency care.

4. An EMT, Jason Tremor (Roanoke Fire Department; #3435; cell phone: 000-000-0000), arrived at 2:52 p.m., examined the laceration to Alice's right temple area, tested her reflexes and vision, and examined her wrist. Tremor said Alice would need sutures for the laceration, and he suggested that the head and wrist be x-rayed as a precaution.

5. At 3:10 p.m., Alice was transported to Roanoke Memorial for further examination and treatment.

6. There was work stoppage for ten minutes from 2:43 to 2:53 p.m. No equipment was damaged.

7. Dr. Aaron Flex, emergency room physician at Roanoke Memorial, put three sutures in Alice's right temple at 3:50 p.m.

8. An X-ray of Alice's head and right wrist revealed no further injuries. (See EMT and hospital reports, attached.)

9. Alice was cleared to return to work the following day.

Further Action

The Safety Department is analyzing the accident further but makes these initial findings:

- Alice Jitters was in violation of the requirement to wear her approved assembly-line shoes.
- Bottled water was positioned by Alice Jitters inside the restricted assembly line area, and this was the direct cause of the accident.

Recommendations

- Safety-rule adherence needs to be more closely monitored and enforced within the assembly-line area.
- Safety rules should be posted in the assembly-line area and reviewed with employees each quarter.
- A reward system for safety-rule compliance should be initiated.

ANNUAL REPORT

The first and most vital point in writing the annual report is knowing who your readers are. They are not only sophisticated investors but also the hourly wage employees who own stock in the company. And the annual report is also an important marketing tool, offering the public an inside view of the organization, its products, profits, and prospects.

So when a big portion of your audience is unknown, it's important to write for every reader—comprehensible and clear; simple, but not simplistic.

Read a number of annual reports prepared by organizations like yours. You can review the winning annual reports from businesses around the world at http://www.mercommawards.com/arc.htm, or go to www.annualreports.com to look at a great variety. You may also go directly to the organizations' Web sites and read them there.

You'll notice that in nearly every case, the language is simple and straightforward, with the theme and the tone being set right on the cover. Here's the cover copy of the Wells Fargo annual report for 2013:

The right people. The right markets. The right model.
Servicing customers in the real economy.

The second page opens with:

Serving customers in the real economy.
What is the real economy? It's the first-time homebuyer looking to buy a home. It's the bookkeeper who needs to make a deposit quickly. It's the veterinarian who sees her business growing. And it's large companies, too—like a family business that is one of the largest growers and suppliers of produce in the U.S.

Wells Fargo's Mindi Weber, who has a background in agriculture, works side by side with customers like Fowler Packing Co. every day on products and services, from its line of credit to treasury management. Co-owner Dennis Parnagian—whose father founded Fowler Packing in 1950—said, "Wells Fargo 'gets it.' They understand our world and our specific needs and challenges. Wells Fargo has shown me it is committed to agriculture and has the personnel and capabilities to do the job right." To Weber, and all Wells Fargo team members, that means developing deep relationships, understanding and serving customers' needs, and helping them succeed financially.

This simple theme is consistent throughout. The letter from the chairman, president, and chief executive officer, John G. Stumpf, begins:

To Our Owners,
2013 was another great year thanks to the dedication of our more than 264,000 team members working together toward our common vision: To satisfy all our customers' financial needs and help them succeed financially.

Our focus on serving customers drove outstanding results. In 2013, Wells Fargo generated record earnings for the fifth consecutive year—in fact, we were the most profitable U.S. bank—and ranked as the world's most valuable bank by market capitalization.

The report continues:

We believe banking—and Wells Fargo—is at its best when supporting the "real economy" by creating new jobs, helping businesses grow, and promoting the financial well-being of individuals. For us, this means keeping deposits safe, lending responsibly and fairly, helping students pay for college and customers plan for their financial futures, supplying needed capital to businesses of all sizes, and investing in communities. It also means instilling confidence in our customers as their financial partner—from providing checking accounts and automobile loans to treasury management and investment banking services.

Here's how Virginia M. Rometty, chairman, president, and chief executive officer at IBM, started her letter to stockholders in the 2013 annual report, following a cover that reads, "What will we make of this moment?"

Dear IBM Investor:
What will we make of this moment—as businesses, as individuals, as societies?
 What will we make with a planet generating unprecedented amounts of data? What will we create from—and with—global networks of consumers, workers, citizens, students, patients? How will we make use of powerful business and technology services available on demand? How will we engage with an emerging global culture, defined not by age or geography, but by people determined to change the practices of business and society?
 To capture the potential of this moment, IBM is executing a bold agenda. It is reshaping your company, and we believe it will reshape our industry. In this letter I will describe the actions we have taken and are taking, and the changed company that is emerging from this transformation. I believe that if you understand our strategy, you will share our confidence in IBM's prospects—for the near term, for this decade and beyond.
 Let's start with the phenomenon of our age—data.

RESEARCH. After reviewing previous annual reports for your organization, talk to the management personnel responsible for supplying parts of the new report. Ask them what they would like to have included and discuss the timeline for getting information submitted.

SCOPE AND BUDGET. Establish the scope of the report, the objectives, the budget you have to produce it, and the timetable for getting it produced. Get management agreement and approval for the budget; also get management input and agreement, often from the chairman and/ or CEO, about the theme, tone, and what to highlight and emphasize.

STRUCTURE. Most annual reports go far beyond meeting the minimal financial reporting requirements and include the following sections:

- **Shareholders' letter.** Set the theme and tone with a direct statement from the president, chairman of the board, and/or CEO. The letter gives an overview of the year's performance, interprets that performance, explains any failures, and indicates future direction.

- **Financial highlights.** Briefly review, in broad strokes, sales and profits for the year, comparing them to those of the previous year, or several years.

- **Narrative section.** In positive terms, cover operations for the year, new products, and developments in the marketplace. Consider including:

  - ▶ Leading profit factors
  - ▶ Market share and performance of current products or services
  - ▶ New products or services
  - ▶ Stock dividends
  - ▶ Productivity
  - ▶ Profit changes
  - ▶ Competitive comparisons
  - ▶ Organizational changes
  - ▶ Forecast outlook for next year
  - ▶ Acquisitions
  - ▶ Restructuring
  - ▶ Research and development
  - ▶ Marketplace trends and changes
  - ▶ Social responsibilities (community service, environmental activities and considerations)

● **Financial statement.** Aimed at showing a complete picture of the organization's financial health, this section needs to be written in direct and clear terms. It should include:

▶ Balance sheet
▶ Income statement
▶ Profit and loss statement (changes in financial position)
▶ Independent auditor's statement
▶ Explanatory footnotes

● **Board of directors and officers.** Include a complete listing of the organization's board of directors and their organizational affiliations. You may also want to include a brief statement about each member and his photograph. The list of organization officers may include the president, vice-presidents, treasurer, and sometimes general managers of divisions. Brief descriptions of areas of responsibility may be included, too.

17

Proposals and Grant Applications That Get Approved

One of the most skilled authors I know told me that she is studying the art of grant writing. Really? Why? There are two reasons: grant writing—proposal writing—demands a very specialized set of *persuasive writing* skills, and each set of RFPs (request for proposals) has unique requirements and rules for applying for grants and awards.

As a proposal writer, you must be able to "sell" your ideas.

Never are the skills of writing well for business success more on the line than they are when you write a proposal to persuade your top managers to approve a plan; to convince a potential client that your ideas and ability to execute them are the best for their needs; or to assure a government agency or a foundation that your organization or you should be awarded a contract or grant because you correctly diagnosed a problem or identified a need and have the right solution and plan, and the capabilities to do what you propose.

Never are the stakes higher, and never are the rewards greater. So, the best approach and first step is to do the complete and thorough *background work* before you begin the writing phase. It's a winner-takes-all challenge, and a one-shot opportunity.

When I ran an advertising, marketing, and public relations agency, my organization's existence hinged on being able to write proposals that won clients over. Everything was on the line each time I went out with a proposal in hand and made a client presentation. That day was often preceded by weeks, even months, of long hours worked by a team of highly skilled experts—from financial estimators to marketing whizzes to gifted graphic artists. And the most critical part of the proposal process was analyzing and evaluating the opportunity and the audience for my proposal.

START WITH RESEARCH

The first vital step in any proposal process is to thoroughly examine the RFP, the grant application requirements, or the business need or problem you propose to solve. Determine early if you should pursue the opportunity. You may find that you can't qualify to bid, for example, or that the terms of the RFP or application simply aren't acceptable to you or your organization. You may find that an organization has preselected a contractor and is simply going through the motions of receiving additional bids because of some legal or organizational requirement.

In the case of writing a proposal (bid) for winning a government contract or securing a business contract, your organization may have to meet financial and insurance-coverage requirements that are beyond your organization's reach.

Be sure you understand all these requirements in detail. If you have questions, inquire. Sometimes you'll find that the RFP is unclear and/ or proposals that don't strictly measure up may still be considered because of a scarcity of bids (or the ineptitude of the RFP writer). Be sure to seek clarification from the awarding organization.

Follow up this examination with a thorough study of the proposals or grants the organization, agency, or foundation has approved or funded in the past. This will give you an idea of their mind-set and preferences.

Ask how many proposals or applications the organization expects will compete (how many invitations to bid they issued) and the number of awards that will be given to get a handle on your real chance of success.

Again, you may decide at this point that you can't or don't want to invest more effort in developing a proposal that has very little or no chance of succeeding. If you can examine past winning proposals, by all means scrutinize them closely and try to learn how satisfied the grantor was with the results.

Also, complete as much research as possible on the people who will be making the decision. This will give you a possible edge, if you know the grant or award committee members or judges and their individual preferences for the types of proposals they favor. If it's ethically possible, network your way to one or more of these people and ask any questions you may have about proposal content or the process. Or, in the case of a grant for something like a new educational program, ask what the funding organization is predisposed to fund for the upcoming awards. And ask staff members. They are often a very valuable source of information.

Meticulous attention to each step in proposal preparation can make all the difference. This is particularly true of the process of winning the bid for new client business; it's also true of being successful in receiving grant funds.

If you decide you're well suited to the opportunity, buckle your seat belt and start the next step.

STUDY THE PROBLEM; COME UP WITH A SOLUTION

The most vital step in the process is studying the problem in depth to come up with the best solution. This can require weeks or months, and a huge investment of time and resources. It will definitely demand brainstorming among your organization's key personnel and getting everyone's best creative input. A construction company, for example, bidding a building modification and remodel will have architects come up with designs, production managers compute labor costs, estimators compute material costs and licensing and other fees, etc.

THINK THROUGH YOUR ENTIRE PROPOSAL

Be sure to brainstorm questions the client may have about your organization or how you will complete all phases of a project. Be sure you can satisfactorily answer any question the client may have. You want to leave no doubt in the client's mind that you can do what you're proposing.

To build your most persuasive case, think through your proposal from beginning to end and make notes until you can state it in one simple purpose or benefits sentence. Focus on how your proposal fulfills a need or provides a solution. In the case of writing an application for a literary grant, for example, your purpose will be based on what you will accomplish in the grant period that's being funded.

Here's how you might start a business proposal for a company that's overwhelmed by the negative effect production waste is having on their profits:

> Wazoo Company will, in one year, reduce Excess's 37% production waste problem to 7% by instituting a three-phase program, "You're Up," consisting of these parts: (1) an employee education program; (2) a bonus-for-savings campaign; and (3) a recycling-the-planet program—all on a budget of $550,000.

Here's how I started my book proposal for this book:

> This little book is your ticket to making it big in business by *writing well*. It will help you

> - Distill your message into a well-targeted statement
> - Write what you want to say, quickly and effectively
> - Ace those elements of style
> - Slam-dunk the essential points of grammar and punctuation
> - Master the tricks of editing yourself

> All with ease and panache. And there are extra pointers here for writing

> - Emails
> - Résumés
> - Reports
> - Proposals
> - Business Plans
> - Presentations
> - Letters

Here are the opening statements of several of the 2014 winning proposals for the annual Alicia Patterson Award, which was set up in 1965 to honor Alicia Patterson, the founding editor and publisher of *Newsday*. The fellowships are the oldest writing fellowships in journalism and are given to print journalists so they can take off six months to a year from their regular jobs to write an in-depth story. The aim is to improve print journalism.

Proposal Title: "A Look at the New Economics and Inequities of Modern Fishing," by Lee van der Voo.

It's a case of the big fish eating the little one. As larger owners and corporations move into fisheries, small boats and their crews are disappearing. This (project) will examine consolidation trends across the 17 existing catch shares in the U.S., weaving the tale around the nation's oldest catch share program. This fishery has consolidated to just a few boats in 22 years, displacing almost an entire labor force of non-vessel-owning captains and crew.

Proposal Title: "Shadow Wars: The Era of Freelance Soldiers and Special Operations Forces," by Kristina Shevory.

The old way the United States goes to war is dead. No longer will the U.S. field hundreds of thousands of soldiers in two large-scale land wars as it did in Afghanistan and Iraq over the last decade. No longer will there be forward operating bases for tens of thousands of soldiers in a battle zone. No longer will the U.S. ship billions of dollars of equipment, housing and material to set up small cities abroad. Instead, the new American way of war will be one fought largely in the shadows.

Proposal Title: "Revisiting Appalachia," by Builder Levy.

What began as a ten-day trip for me in 1968 became fourteen years of visiting and photographing in coal mines, miners' homes and communities in the hills and "hollers" of West Virginia, eastern Kentucky, southwestern Virginia, and western Pennsylvania. My initial focus was on the Appalachian coal miner.

I had been attracted by the miners' tradition for more than a century of collective struggle to make life better for themselves, their families and the American working people. I was interested in the earlier Appalachian Mountain people's heritage, which included escaping from and resistance to British colonial rule, the Underground Railroad and abolitionism.

Today, the key issues in Central Appalachia still revolve around coal, but mainly in the relationship to the environment. I want to revisit Appalachia not only to extend my previous work on miners, and the coalfield communities, but also to focus on the environmental issues that are threatening the very existence of these communities.

**Proposal Title: "Divided We Stand: Making Sense of America's New Multinational Identity,"
by Frances Stead Sellers.**

Ten years ago, I walked into the Edward A. Garmatz Federal Courthouse in downtown Baltimore and swore, as every new American citizen must, to "renounce and adjure all allegiance and fidelity to any foreign prince, potentate, state or sovereignty of whom or which I have heretofore been a subject or citizen."

Several weeks later, when I flew back to London to visit my family, I left my new American passport in my bag and handed my worn British document to the immigration officer. That's what I've done ever since, changing my identity each time I cross the frontier from American visitor to homecoming Brit.

Am I a hypocrite? Perhaps. I've never been entirely comfortable with my double life. But I'm hardly alone. I am one of a growing number of dual citizens—Americans whose lingering psychological ties to our mother countries are reinforced by the passports we still carry and the citizenships we still hold. For most of us, the decision to maintain these ties is sanctioned by our governments. . . .

I would use an Alicia Patterson Fellowship to explore the phenomenon of divided loyalties and what it means in a world in which human migration and globalized communications have created not only multicultural but also multinational communities.

OUTLINE WITH PURPOSE

Outline your proposal carefully, following the RFP or application format to the letter. Be sure you cover all the essential information, including:

- ▶ Introduction / summary / statement of purpose
- ▶ Proposal description or narrative (project description and scope; budget, or how grant funds will be used; schedule of phases or tasks; project outcomes)
- ▶ Organization description (personnel assignments, organization capabilities, and prior similar projects)
- ▶ Conclusion or outcomes
- ▶ Supporting materials (appendixes, licenses, résumés)

INFUSE WITH ENTHUSIASM

While it may seem incongruous to say that your proposal for a government project should show some passion, as well as a logical and comprehensive approach, it's true. Passion or enthusiasm must show through. Demonstrate that you and your organization are eager—but not overly eager or desperate—for the opportunity. In the case of a grant application, this translates into being a motivated and worthy candidate.

You must show that you have the answers, or can get them, and that you've thought through your proposal, have weighed and anticipated the problems, have the resources or wherewithal, and are confident that you have the solutions to carry the project to a successful conclusion. You must sell the audience on the fact that you, or your organization, are the right candidate for the project.

START WITH CONFIDENCE

After your purpose statement, write a first paragraph that illuminates the problem to be solved, your proposed solution, and what you will accomplish if granted the contract or funding. If research is part of your proposal, very briefly describe it here, too. And be sure to include all of your and your organization's pertinent credentials. Include information such as how long your company has been in business, your annual sales and financial resources, references from satisfied customers and clients, and your insurance coverage.

KEEP TO THE POINT

In the body of your proposal, or the narrative, use subheads, bullets, and concise writing to lead your audience through each step of the project, including the approach and methods that will be used, the budget required, and the schedule for completion. Start with the statement of *need* or a *case statement*, if more expansion and explanation is required beyond your purpose statement. Be sure you clearly state *why* and *how* your proposal is the answer to the problem or need and emphasize the benefits of your approach and methods of execution. Most RFPs will have questions or sections into which this information must be entered.

To demonstrate that you went beyond your competitors, include a Q&A that answers any questions your audience might have about your organization's capabilities and the thoroughness with which you prepared your proposal. But don't include anything extraneous. Keep the writing tight and focused. This isn't a game of the longest entry wins.

FINISH STRONG

Make a convincing statement about the project outcomes. Include a comprehensive picture of what the funding organization will get—or can expect in the case of a grant—as a result of the work performed by you or your organization. Use terms of quantifiable results—state the exact improved function and beauty after your building remodel, or a completed book on health care improvements, in the case of grant funding for a year. Be as specific as possible, and include objective facts and figures when you can.

CALL FOR ACTION

End with a strong call to action or build in some urgency. You may decide to offer, for example, an incentive if the business proposal is signed within thirty days. This can be explained by stating that your company is prepared to offer a 5 percent discount in order to be able to schedule upcoming work. And you will want to build in an expiration date for the proposal to encourage the decision-making process. (An expiration date is almost always necessary when bidding things like a construction project, because material and labor prices can increase.)

You may want the urgency to be more pointed. For example, if you are proposing to a corporation that they fund a Big Brothers project for the coming year, explain that without funding, the program won't happen.

ADD THE PIZZAZZ

Once you are satisfied that your proposal is comprehensive and concise, don't be afraid to add a bit of flavor, or a light touch or two—using the knowledge you acquired about the organization you're proposing to and the people who will be reading your proposal and making the decision. This is an optional step that can work very well, but it must be done with extreme care. If in doubt, don't.

Round up a few expert and objective readers to review the final draft of your proposal and offer comments. The more like your intended audience your reviewers are, the better their review results will be. When the stakes are high—like that multimillion-dollar contract your organization is trying to land—don't rush the final stages of editing, reviewing, and proofreading. Be sure to catch all small errors and typos. Details matter and will be judged. And don't forget the step of making it as visually appealing as possible. Photos, renderings, graphs, tables, and illustrations can add the kind of pizzazz that sells clients.

But the real proof is always in the writing. That is what will get your proposal read with interest and allow it to rise to the top of the candidate pile. And the writing is what will put you or your organization in the winner's circle.

18

The Presentation That Gets the Contract

When you are elected to be the presenter of the proposal to a potential client, your "stage" will undoubtedly be a boardroom, and your "audience" will be the officers of the potential client company. Your "props" for this performance will be the assembled and bound hard-copy proposals, which your potential client may have received and reviewed well in advance. You may also elect to use a PowerPoint or other visual or audiovisual program to convey part or all of your message. You may have some other props, too. Maybe for a large remodel or a brand-new construction project you will have architectural renderings displayed on large easels and samples of building materials—from glossy granites to space-age weather-strong siding—for an opportunity to give more substance and hands-on elements. You may also have arranged to have expert walk-ons from your staff or members of outside organizations.

You'll want the presentation to be conversational and informal; yet you'll want a level of spit and polish that makes it clear that you are a professional and that your organization has labored long and hard to create a very well-thought-out and comprehensive proposal. So, what should you do? How should you prepare? Or should you just "wing it"?

KNOW THE AUDIENCE

"Well," you might ask, "isn't that obvious; and haven't you covered this point ad nauseam?" Maybe. But let's do it again. The better you know the individuals you'll be presenting to, the better your chances of selling them on your proposal. And even though you know Jim Martin is the CFO, Jack Sprat is the CEO, and Eggy Drop is the COO, you will help yourself a great deal if you know that Jim has a passion for golf and shoots two over par nearly every Saturday morning at the Bruiser Club; Jack has a black and tan coonhound he treats like a child and dresses up for Halloween; and Eggy hates anything that's colored yellow. Not only should you have used this information during the proposal-writing stage, it will be invaluable during the small-talk, ice-breaking minutes before the presentation. Use it and get everyone comfortable.

TAKE CONTROL

Whether you're still in the boardroom or you're standing before an audience of thousands at the Met, you will need to have a plan, have practiced it until it's smooth and flawless, and have done a run-through (or more than one) with any walk-on participants. Leave nothing to chance. You'll gain confidence by being superprepared.

YOU'RE READY WHEN YOU:

- ▶ Can answer any questions that may arise.
- ▶ Know and have heard what each presenter will say, and how he will say it.
- ▶ Have given each presenter a time limit. The presentations should be very short. If you have concerns about anyone's ability to make his contribution, do it yourself, and have the expert stand by for questions.
- ▶ Have made sure each presenter has rehearsed his contribution. (Tell each person that you're timing him and how much time he has, and that you will signal him when he has one minute to wrap up.)
- ▶ Have any special equipment set up and tested.

START WITH THE CLIENT'S PROBLEM OR NEED

Nothing will demonstrate that you understand what you're doing more than starting with a clear statement of the client's need or problem. If you can cite research findings and figures to bolster this statement, all the better. This will make the client relax, and with your show of confidence, the client company will believe that it is in good hands and that your organization is capable of delivering the right solution and benefits.

ORGANIZE FOR UNDERSTANDING

Following the structure and points of your proposal will ensure that your audience can easily understand your message. Using an audiovisual aid can be effective, but you may elect to use only a copy of the proposal itself to keep the presentation conversational. Or you may tell your audience that each person will receive a copy of the proposal at the end of the meeting, so they aren't distracted by riffling through the pages or taking copious notes.

LAY OUT YOUR PRESENTATION PLAN

Tell your audience what you're going to tell them; then tell them; and finish by telling them what you told them. Then ask for the contract. You might say something like, "I want to walk you through the proposal in the next thirty minutes, and then we'll take any questions you may still have." You may introduce the walk-on experts who will be presenting information to bolster your proposal and who will be on tap to answer questions during the Q&A segment.

STAY ON TARGET

Deliver exactly what you promised, and do so precisely on time. No one loves a presenter who's fifty-eight minutes into his thirty-minute presentation and shows no signs of winding down. That presenter will have lost most or all of his credibility and probably all of his audience.

A light note or two may ease any tension in the room, but don't let the focus wander, and don't digress or lapse into any extraneous material. Once this happens, things can unravel quickly, and getting back on track can be difficult. And while you may believe that humor is the great icebreaker, that's true only if the person delivering it has the special performance genes of a real comedian. (If you decide to go with humor, make it very brief and self-deprecating. Don't chance anything that could be misinterpreted or seem off-color.) The serious, well-prepared, and competent presenter is just as appreciated. (For every person who enjoys a joke, there are twenty people who much prefer a serious, concise, and clear presentation.)

KEEP THE "YOU" FOCUS

Frame and execute your presentation with a "you" focus. That means start with the client's problem or needs and continue with a client-centered solution. List the benefits. Even in presenting your organization's qualifications, credentials, and successful work examples, focus on how these things meet the client's needs and on the benefits these things bring to the client's project. For example, state that you are qualified to do an excellent job on the remodel of their offices because you demonstrated those capabilities in completing the remodel of the Nerd and Geek offices on the other side of town—that organization's needs and challenges were similar to the client's. "Having Squat and Square as our legal team means you will have all potential legal issues anticipated and dealt with in a timely manner, which will avoid any possible construction delays."

PRESENT LIKE A PRO

Stand up straight, make eye contact, and smile. It's infectious. It makes the audience relax. It makes you relax.

Ask if everyone can hear you. And if you're using a video screen, ask if everyone can see.

It's far better to keep the room bright and airy and slightly cool—especially in the afternoon—so everyone remains alert.

Look at your audience while you speak, not at a screen, if you're using one. And use the heads and subheads used in the written proposal so your audience is never lost. (Write heads and subheads that reflect the content and underscore your points, not ones that name the proposal sections. Don't use "Introduction"; use "Bark and Muzzle Needs New Digs." Don't use "Conclusions"; use "Happy Dogs and Happy Best Friends.")

After you read a heading, give your pointed explanation; pause; then move to the next point. Watch the audience for signs of interest and attention. If John seems distracted or is texting, engage him with "John, I think you'll agree that this point is vital . . ." If Jack is disruptive, fidgeting, or checking email, you might insert a light note with "Did I mention there'll be a quiz?" to tactfully let him know his full attention will be appreciated.

Keep it conversational and relaxed, and everyone will have a better experience.

BRING ON THE PIZZAZZ

Use a sparse number of graphs, illustrations, and charts, and make sure they are right on point. Don't try to dazzle with flashing photos, dissolving charts, dancing illustrations, and music building to a crescendo in the background. These aren't things that will deliver the message you're trying to get across, unless maybe you're trying to sell a new Web site program or a film project.

Coming up with a "take-away" item that underscores your message can be worthwhile. Maybe a carpenter's rule that's very useful and bears your logo. But gimmicks and giveaways often just say that your organization is willing to waste money and that you perhaps doubt whether your proposal is strong enough to win the contract on its own.

ASK FOR THE CONTRACT

There's always a delicate balance between finishing strong and decisively, and then asking for the contract, and finishing in a hard-sell mode that turns off the audience. Don't be shy, and don't let the Q&A segment drift and trail off without a strong conclusion that asks for the contract. Keep your tone conversational and upbeat, but don't forget to *close*. Your organization may be one in a line of several or more that will be pitching the potential client, so you want it and your presentation to be memorable. And you want the business.

Restate, very briefly, the *benefits* of selecting your organization and ask for the deal. It will undoubtedly have to be ad lib, but be prepared to say something like "Now we've shown you how XYZ can do a top-notch job for Bark and Muzzle, can we sign the contract?" Or "Now that we've answered all your remaining questions, let's do the deal." "I know you agree that XYZ offers you everything you want in this remodel, plus added benefits, so let's make it happen, and sign the contract." "I believe the benefits of working with XYZ to achieve your goals have been demonstrated. We're eager to get started. Let's sign the contract."

19

The Speech That Gets Applause

Many points of making a presentation also apply to making a speech, but there are some differences.

Stand up, say what you have to say, and sit down. Wasn't that the advice given to a reticent and self-conscious Eleanor Roosevelt when she was being urged to go out and make speeches to help keep the Roosevelt name in the public consciousness? Sounds easy enough. But for your speech to be both moving and memorable—as if you are having a frank heart-to-heart conversation with a single person—you'll need to do some careful and thorough preparation before you push back your chair and get to your feet.

DECIDE ON A THEME, A SUBJECT, A TITLE

If the topic is assigned, you've got this covered. But chances are you will have a clean slate (and an open microphone), and all you will know is that your speech is to be one that inspires. Or persuades. So, it's time to decide on a theme and then come up with a title for your speech— make it lively and engaging.

The title needs to tell the audience something about the content. And it needs to "hook" them with a bit of intrigue. Think in terms of headlines and keep it short. Use numbers (which you'll use in the speech) or ask a question. Words like "power," "magic," "steps," "how to," "secret," and "miracle" have been used to good effect. Take a look at a few leading historical speech titles and note how they give you an idea of what the speaker covered:

- ▶ "Farewell to Baseball," Lou Gehrig
- ▶ "Address to the Nation on the *Challenger*," Ronald Reagan
- ▶ "We Shall Fight on the Beaches," Winston Churchill
- ▶ "Duty, Honor, Country," Douglas MacArthur

You'll go for something with pizzazz, but don't forget to include something of the subject, too. And keep that firmly in mind as you write. You need to deliver on it.

In thinking about the speeches that have impressed you, you will probably recall that there were characteristics that made them memorable: the speaker used a conversational tone; made only one to four points; built the talk carefully, one point on another; and repeated each point at least several times. Maybe the speaker used a brief audience-participation prop to get things rolling, raise the energy level in the room, and get the audience's attention. Even a show of hands with a question or, for a boomer crowd, something like, "Remember these three phrases . . . There'll be a quiz, a winner, and a prize at the end." Whatever you decide to use, if anything, make it simple and very brief.

MAKE IT PERSONAL

Build on your title. Since you've chosen one that promises to be memorable, carefully and logically hang your speech on it. Think of it as the trunk of a tree and your points as its limbs, your subpoints as its smaller branches. Keep everything connected, and keep the lifeblood of your speech flowing. Don't branch far from the trunk, and don't plant any extraneous shrubs along the way.

While this may be a command appearance for your audience, don't let yourself off the hook. Make your speech personal and engaging. And infuse it with enthusiasm. The personal appeal of the speaker, personal stories and illustrations, and a message that the audience can take personally make for a very good speech.

LEAP RIGHT IN

With your first draft finished, read it aloud and listen for that conversational quality. And listen for what you can cut. You will hear what needs to go and what needs to be rewritten. Cut any long introductory thanks and credits beyond the very minimum necessary. If you must include any, make them brief, pause, and dive in.

The best speech length is twenty minutes or less, so whittle what you have to say down to that length of time. Keep your take-away message in mind as you read. Start with it, repeat it, and end with it.

Repeat your main points and illustrate them with interesting examples. But be sure not to belabor them or trail off course. Think of your speech as a circle. You want to end where you started.

PRACTICE, PRACTICE, PRACTICE

Now it's time to practice out loud. Time yourself as you begin. Practice until you get a pleasing pace and rhythm. Edit or add material.

Practice in front of a mirror to see how you look, and record yourself on a tape recorder or on video so you can hear and see where you need to improve eye contact, gestures, voice modulation, or speed of delivery. Check to see if you need to gain a more natural pose or improve your facial expressions. Is the person you see and hear someone who would hold your attention if you were in the audience? Are you smiling—or at least not grimacing?

Most speakers will be more comfortable going over their speeches until they can deliver them with just a few notes on a sheet, on note cards, or from cues on a teleprompter (or your computer). But if you feel more at ease having the entire speech written out, use a highlighter and capitalization to allow you to comfortably look at your audience, and then glance at your speech as you need to.

END ON A HIGH NOTE

End with your theme and with something that underscores your take-away message and reinforces your one to four major points. Make sure it's a high note that crowns your message, inspires, persuades, or calls to action.

20

The Résumé That Gets the Interview

The most important thing to know about your résumé is that it's a tool-box from which you must craft a unique, well-targeted document for each job opening. Take this approach whenever you learn about a position you'd like to apply for or whenever you find a job listing on an organization's job board, other job boards, or networking Web sites like Monster or LinkedIn.

Crafting a new résumé for each new opportunity means extra work. But just like each position is unique, so should your résumé be written and arranged to best showcase your skills for a specific job.

This lets you position yourself as the right answer for the problem the employer is trying to solve. And when you apply online—which is the way 97 percent of employers now find candidates to interview—lard your résumé with relevant keywords from the ad and the ones you find on the organization's Web site. This will improve your chances of having the screening software, the automated applicant tracking system (ATS), select your résumé or application as a possible candidate. Scoring high here and on application questions can place your résumé at the top of the candidate list.

Don't be creative when applying online. Follow the format exactly. Yes, you want to communicate your work experience, education, special skills, achievements, and maybe career objectives—and, infrequently, a little personal information—but do it in the prescribed format. Some screening software confuses information like your employer and your job title if they are not arranged correctly and consistently, so put those things on separate lines, and in the prescribed order. Some ATSs also get confused over the use of abbreviations and bullets. Check this out, and follow instructions. Also, be precise about your specific skills. ATSs give extra points for the ones the employer wants, so list them by their proper names, like UNIX, Java, Power-Point, etc.

And, as a last stop before you start tailoring your submission, go to the organization's Web site and look for the values, goals, and creed statements. You'll want to include any of those terms that fit your experience and interests. For example, include a personal interests section and list your green project volunteer work if the company you're applying to emphasizes environmental sustainability, like one of the *Forbes* leaders listed for 2014, Westpac Banking (based in Sydney), Biogen Idec, Samsung Electronics, Coca-Cola, L'Oréal, Johnson & Johnson, or Nissan.

Some organizations assign added points for things like top-tier universities. If you've even taken adult education courses at one of these schools, list them. And if there's the possibility of amending your application with additional keywords, do it.

If you follow these pointers and don't receive an invitation for an interview, don't be discouraged. This may not be a reflection on you and your listed qualifications. Organizations often have preselected an employee for the spot and are advertising only to meet fair-hiring-practices regulations by soliciting outside candidates. Other times, organizations are just testing the candidate pool. And there are occasions when organizations advertise a position opening, then change their mind, or are just too disorganized to conduct the selection and hiring steps. All these factors are reasons why you must be diligent, apply for as many openings as possible, and initiate your own search with organizations you target as desirable workplaces. Develop your own strategy, work hard, and use the following steps to get the job you want.

GIVE YOURSELF THE BEST CHANCE

It's still true that the best chance of landing your dream job comes by way of an employee recommending you for the position—preferably an employee at the upper-management level with an outstanding reputation. Use this approach, if you can. And network through your professional associations, alumni groups, and personal contacts to make it happen. No one will think you are bending the rules of friendship if you mention that you're searching for a new position and would appreciate any leads they may hear about. (But don't refer to an employee within the organization you're applying to without the person's express permission.)

Network directly with organizations to get the inside track on positions coming open and to learn exactly what the employer is looking for in candidates to fill these positions. Do a thorough study of the organization, starting with its Web site. Call and inquire of the human resources department (HR). Learn the name of the person who has the power to hire and, if possible, make a personal contact through your professional association, a business associate, or a networking Web site like LinkedIn. Then start to hone your résumé carefully to show that you are the solution to the employer's problem.

Consider asking for an exploratory interview or speaking with HR and the manager(s) about future needs. This is difficult, mind-numbing work, and it can be very discouraging, but it can also turn up opportunities. So stick with it. In an electronic world, you can gain special traction if you carefully use strategies of personal contact.

GO WITH YOUR STRENGTHS

Should you always lead by listing your experience first? Should you include an objective, especially if you're just starting out? Is there a place for special interests or personal information?

The answer to the first question is organize your résumé by *starting with your greatest strengths*. What does that mean? If you've just graduated from college and have only unrelated summer job experience or did an unrelated internship, for example, lead with your *education*— unless the ad invites beginners or your internship is very impressive.

If you write an *objective*, use keywords from the ad and organization Web site that relate directly to the position for which you're applying.

In the *experience* section, list those jobs that demonstrate your leadership qualities, work ethic, skill set, and dedication to a cause, a charity, or volunteer work.

Try to match the ad keywords wherever possible, focusing on your transferable personal skills. (If you're unclear about these, complete your own personal evaluation, like the ones presented in the résumé chapter of my book *How to Write It* and in Richard Bolles's *What Color Is Your Parachute?*) There are lots of opportunities for bright young talent. Also, demonstrate a great attitude in your objective statement (if you use one).

BRAINSTORM

Study the ad and match up your skills and demonstrated experience— your expertise that offers solutions and benefits to the organization. Think in terms of accomplishments with hard facts and numbers, not in terms of job descriptions.

- ▶ What experience or skills do you have that are named in the ad?
- ▶ What have you been able to learn from the organization's Web site that you should use as words to emphasize?

Make your list using powerful action verbs. Think in terms of quantifiable accomplishments.

Now, go back through your list and delete articles, personal pronouns ("I"), and adjectives and adverbs. You probably have six seconds, TheLadders research reports, to capture your reader's interest, so make every word count.

Edit what you've written. Make sure it is: (1) relevant to the position; (2) clearly stated in powerful, action verbs; and (3) concise, without extra descriptive words.

Make a complete skills listing. Many application processes want this information listed; it's often the foremost consideration in qualifying applicants.

DEVELOP YOUR RÉSUMÉ

List your last four jobs, or about ten to fifteen years of employment. Start with the most recent and work backward. Don't leave time gaps;

explain periods of absence from the workforce with skill-related statements, like "Created and managed successful $500,000 end-of-life plan for ninety-year-old parent." Use up to five distinct results for each position you held and list results in concrete terms of facts and figures. Focus on how the results you have listed relate to your career future with statements like:

- Increased production by 20% over six months by eliminating four clerical steps.

- Increased, by 32%, 500 new employees' production by planning, writing, and administering orientation program.

Remember the golden rule: do not exaggerate, distort the facts, embellish, or lie. And don't use trickery, like including keywords in white type, to game the AST. Don't include statements that cast you in a negative light. And don't be modest or shy, either. State clearly and succinctly your best attributes without a braggart or flippant tone.

Start with your most powerful statements, and keep them concise and simple.

BUILD YOUR FINAL RÉSUMÉ

Create a clean, open, and visually appealing document (though application forms often require cutting and pasting your résumé pieces, and your formatting may be lost).

There are three types of formats you may use: *chronological,* where typically you list your experience at the top (after your objective, if you elect to use one) and start with most recent experience; *functional,* which presents your skill areas; and *creative,* which can use a combination of format elements to show your skills in the most powerful way. See the examples at the end of the chapter and decide which will work best for you.

If you are required to use an application form, you may still be able to submit your résumé as an attachment. And if you know the person who has the power to hire you for the position, mail or email a copy (or both) to that person.

SELECT A FORMAT

- Select a professional-looking typeface (font). Consider Helvetica, Times New Roman, New Century Schoolbook, Arial, Tahoma, or Calibri. Don't combine styles.

- Aim to put your résumé on a single sheet.

- Don't use headers, footers, or embedded tables, pictures, or other graphics because these can confuse the ATS and eliminate you from being considered for the position.

- Use boldface type, strong italics (many are too delicate), large type, and attention-getting spacing to make your point, if you are sending your résumé directly, or if the ATS allows it. Use boldface type on your subheads and/or other items like name and telephone number, objective or executive summary (if used), job titles, education, and special interests, skills, and licenses (if used) to make these items stand out.

- Use a font of 11 points or larger for easy reading. You may want to use larger type for your most important information.

- Print in black ink for ease of reading and copying.

- Balance your material vertically and horizontally on the page so that it looks open and clean.

- Use the white space to get the reader's attention and draw attention to your main points of emphasis.

- Select a quality paper if you're mailing your résumé. Don't use pastels and "shocking" colors. Test your paper selection to be sure it copies well. (Some heavy papers jam copiers.) Select envelopes that match your résumé paper.

TOP MATERIAL

- Place your name prominently, centered, flush left, or flush right, and use a larger, bold typeface. If you have a common name, use your middle name or initial, and use this consistently everywhere, LinkedIn, Google+, Twitter, Facebook, etc., to create your "brand."

- Below your name, place your contact information. Some recruiters advise not including your home address, just your city and state; one email address; one direct-to-you telephone number; and the URL to your professional online profile. This helps you control communications.

- Never state the salary you are seeking.

OBJECTIVE/EXECUTIVE SUMMARY

- Consider a well-targeted executive summary ("elevator pitch") focused on how you will benefit the hiring organization. Generic statements about professional objectives are usually a waste of space. For many positions, it's best to not include either.

- Limit your statement to three or five concise sentences or statements of your skills, what you're seeking, and how it will benefit (add value to) the organization.

EXPERIENCE

- Think in terms of value to the reader. Emphasize what you can do for the hiring organization.

- Dates of employment can be listed either flush left or flush right. Go for the cleanest and most appealing arrangement.

- List your most recent employer first and include the organization name (but not address), city, and state, starting at the left. Some recruiters advise including a very brief organization description (type of industry) and size immediately below the organization name. This lets the hiring organization get a better handle on your experience.

- Form your accomplishment statements to demonstrate why you are the right person for the job.

- Include two to five points (use bullets, if allowed) for each job. Don't use complete sentences; use telegraphic statements.

- Make each statement in hard-fact-accomplishment terms. Use a result-by-action approach. These facts may be resulting improvements or money saved. "Saved $550,000 in annual labor costs by eliminating three production steps." "Increased annual sales to $2.3 million (22% increase) by creating new training program."

- Keep statements to fifteen words or less. Less is more.

- Eliminate articles ("a," "an," "the") and personal pronouns ("I") from your statements, and don't use a period at the end of each. Edit each to its most concise form.

- Double-space and use white space to draw the reader's eye to important points.

- Use part-time jobs if you are a recent graduate, or the part-time job is very relevant to the position you're seeking.

- Eliminate unnecessary descriptive words like "creative," "innovative," "hard-working," "futuristic," "dedicated," "bottom-line oriented." Dull résumés contain lots of descriptive statements that look like they were copied right out of a corporate personnel manual. Also eliminate vagueness, jargon, and clichés.

EDUCATION / SPECIAL INTERESTS / EXTRACURRICULAR ACTIVITIES / CONTINUING EDUCATION / AWARDS AND HONORS / MEMBERSHIPS AND AFFILIATIONS / PERSONAL / REFERENCES

Think carefully before adding any of these sections beyond the one for education. Include only one of these if there is a strong, relevant reason; and certainly don't include information from high school unless it is very relevant. (If you know the interviewer graduated from your high school, it's worth mentioning.)

If your technical skills rank high on the list of qualifications the hiring organization is looking for, insert a "Skills" or "Key Skills" section at the top of your résumé before your experience. If you've won awards that will uniquely qualify you for the position, list those predominately on your résumé. Remember, lead with your strengths.

- Place education last, unless you are a recent college graduate with less than three years of work experience; then lead with it.

- Limit personal information that is not pertinent to the position.

- Include personal awards or achievements if they are pertinent.

- List current licenses, certificates, and other pertinent qualifications.

- Include professional associations that are important to your career, especially if you held a prominent office. List those that relate to the position you are targeting.

- List any continuing education courses, especially if taken at recognized institutions.

- Don't include references or the statement "References upon request." This is obvious and wastes space.

TAKE A LAST CRITICAL LOOK

- Check to ensure you have no typos. Use the computer spell-checker, but also go over the résumé to catch correctly spelled words that are incorrectly used, like "too" for "to."

- Give the résumé a little breathing time before your final proofing. With just a little shelf time, you'll be able to have a completely fresh, objective look.

- Ask experts in your field or HR to review and comment on your résumé, if you have time.

- Read your résumé aloud. This often helps you identify something you should rewrite.

APPLY IMMEDIATELY

If possible, apply before the opening is actually advertised. Being first is very important. This takes vigilance and a bit of luck. Employers are inundated with résumés and applications—hundreds to thousands for each opening. Procter & Gamble received nearly a million applications for two thousand new positions last year.

Organizations usually begin processing résumés as they receive them. Half of these résumés are eliminated by the ATSs. Then, in medium- or large-sized organizations, HR or recruiters go through the first and top-scoring résumés that remain and select only three or four that seem the most qualified. Only these few candidates are invited for interviews. That means that candidates submitting their résumés even shortly after the job posting goes up may not be considered, or they are considered only after the first candidates have been interviewed and eliminated.

DO YOU NEED A COVER LETTER?

What are the chances your cover letter will be read?

According to leading recruiters, some ATSs do treat cover letters as searchable text, in the same way they treat résumés; but most don't. And most recruiters hired by organizations to fill positions don't even pass cover letters on to hiring managers.

But that doesn't mean that you shouldn't write them. Cover letters are a concise way to restate your value to the organization; and some recruiters, HR personnel, and hiring managers do use them to ferret out candidates. The cover letter can put you in a commanding position. It demonstrates your attention to detail and your ability to analyze the organization's needs and cast yourself in the position.

If you are applying to a small organization that doesn't use an ATS, your cover letter will more likely be read by HR and the hiring manager.

When the ATS stores your cover letter with your résumé as searchable text, those keywords you include will score you points. So use your cover letter to put in additional skills and credentials to add additional searchable keywords that a company may have programmed in the ATS to identify candidates for a specific job.

If your cover letter must be an attachment, recruiters say, it's unlikely that it will be searched and processed like a résumé. Less than 10 percent of HR departments scan cover letters. (Job boards don't scan cover letters, only résumés.)

But don't count those cover letters out, because hiring managers, recruiters report, have denied interviews to candidates qualified by their résumés who didn't submit cover letters.

Here's what to include:

▶ Address the individual who has the power to hire you, whenever possible. When you are applying by mail, and directly, call and find out who this person is.

▶ Make the tone conversational, personal, and direct.

▶ Lead with a "hook." The best type is a personal reference the hiring manager knows or specific information that relates to the organization or industry.

▶ Include specific facts with numbers, if possible.

▶ Lard your letter with keywords from the ad and the organization's Web site.

▶ Use a specific example from your résumé, preferably something that will intrigue the reader and he'll carefully read it.

▶ Propose the next step, if you are contacting the organization directly. Use something like "I will follow up with you next week," "I look forward to discussing details of my experience with you," or "I will be in [city] next week and can come in for an interview on Thursday afternoon. I'll call your office Monday to see if this will work."

▶ Conclude on an upbeat note of anticipation, if possible. "Thank you in advance for your consideration, I look forward to meeting with you." "I look forward to an opportunity to relate in detail what I might add to your outstanding [type] team."

TIPS

Think carefully about how to get the most power and punch into your statements under each category of your résumé. Here are some examples.

Education Examples

- Achieved 4.0 GPA while working twenty hours per week and participating in two sports
- Led staff of twenty-five reporters and increased distribution by 25 percent, as editor of award-winning college newspaper *The Boil*

Special-Interest Examples

- Established Women's Democratic Club; built membership to 1,320 in two years
- Raised $10,500 for reforesting fire-damaged Whittiker Park after organizing "Think Green" spring frolic
- Designed 2014 "Get Moving" program adopted by city of Denver
- Organized 92 percent successful women-in-business managing-your-time seminar for 500 underprivileged women

Training Examples

- Graduated number two from Wharton 2014 effective sales leaders program
- Completed AMA marketing-for-profit workshop
- Graduated first in Xerox sales training program 2014

Military Examples

- Completed airborne training, first out of 94
- Learned conversational German in four months
- Mastered AS-11 guidance system in five months

Community-Activity Examples

- Implemented Meals on Wheels program for 1,500 participants
- Started petition gaining 5,500 signatures against irresponsible mining operations

Family and Household Examples

- Remodeled seven-room house in five months while working full-time
- Established family trust fund for seven siblings
- Managed annual family budget for nine on $56,000 salary

Sport/Hobby Examples

- Designed and built seven-room vacation house on a $150,000 budget in three months
- Organized state tennis tournament for 520 participants
- Improved USTA tennis ability from 2.0 to 4.5 in two months

EXPERT EXAMPLE

As an example of the information you should include in your résumé, examine this biographical statement published in *Forbes* after Virginia Rometty was named IBM president, CEO, and chairman of the board in 2012. There are keys here to expressing your achievements. Think about this: if you were writing Ginni Rometty's résumé, what key questions would you ask her about results that you'd use? Now, apply this to your own résumé writing.

Ginni Rometty is Chairman, President and Chief Executive Officer of IBM. Mrs. Rometty was appointed President and CEO effective January 1, 2012. She became Chairman of the Board of Directors on October 1, 2012.

Mrs. Rometty began her career with IBM in 1981 in Detroit, Michigan. Since then she has held a series of leadership positions in IBM, most recently as Senior Vice President and Group Executive, IBM Sales, Marketing and Strategy. In this role, she was responsible for business results in the 170 global markets in which IBM operates and pioneered IBM's rapid expansion in the emerging economies of the world.

Prior to this, Mrs. Rometty served as Senior Vice President, IBM Global Business Services, where she led the successful integration of PricewaterhouseCoopers Consulting. This acquisition was the largest in professional services history, creating a global team of more than 100,000 business consultants and services experts. In recognition of her leadership in the professional services industry, Mrs. Rometty was honored with the Carl Sloane Award 2006, given by the Association of Management Consulting Firms.

In prior leadership roles, Mrs. Rometty served as general manager of IBM Global Services, Americas, as well as general manager of IBM's Global Insurance and Financial Services Sector.

Mrs. Rometty serves on the Council on Foreign Relations; the Board of Trustees of Northwestern University; and the Board of Overseers and Board of Managers of Memorial Sloan-Kettering Cancer Center.

She holds a Bachelor of Science degree with high honors in computer science and electrical engineering from Northwestern University.

RÉSUMÉ EXAMPLES

Chronological Résumé

Sally Doowell
444-555-6666 Sun City, CA Sallydoowell@jobs.com
URL: SeeMe.com/sallydoowell

AWARD-WINNING PUBLIC AND MEDIA RELATIONS EXECUTIVE
Ad World top honors for national, local, and trade media writing and placement for consumer, financial services, food, and travel products.

EXPERIENCE
Sell Communications | Chicago, IL | 2005–Present
Vice President
Provide media relations and writing service to 40 organizations nationwide
Secured commitments for four feature placements among targeted media in one month
Placed feature stories in seven business magazines for national manufacturer seeking to improve national visibility
Secured positive news coverage in the *Wall Street Journal, Barron's,* Bloomberg Television, *Businessweek, Financial Times, Forbes, Fortune, Investor's Business Daily,* CNBC, and CNN for five publicly traded companies

Shout Advertising and Public Relations | Austin, TX | 2001–2005
Vice President
Successfully increased public relations billings from $40 million to $50 million per year
Oversaw new business development, recruiting, and supervision
Spearheaded, in six months, launch of "Just for Kids" meals that became Jolly's largest brand
Expanded Jolly account to include two additional product lines

Just Right Public Relations | Waco, TX | 1999–2001
Senior Group Manager
Won 14 monthly agency awards for outstanding media placements, supervising three $500,000 annual billing accounts
Promoted five times during tenure

SKILLS
Development: new business, media relations, media training
Media relations: product introductions, targeted media placements, media tours
Project management: publications, special events, vendors, and freelance management
Writing: advertorials, brochures, articles, collateral case histories, marketing materials, newsletters, press kits, press releases, proposals, reports, scripts

AWARDS AND RECOGNITION
PRSA Award of Excellence (Silver Anvil finalist), 2014

EDUCATION
Bachelor of Arts, journalism (with honors), University of Texas, Austin
Certificate of business administration, DePaul, Chicago
Graduate business courses, University of Texas, Austin

Chronological Résumé

Stephen Q. Blank
222-333-4444 StephenQBlank@contact.com
URL:SeeMe.com/StephenQBlank
One First Street, Roanoke, Virginia 00000

EXPERIENCE
Stewart and Zeus | Los Angeles, CA   2009–Present
Vice President
- Completed over 30 midsize corporation due diligence pro formas in 12 months, including quantitative financial analyses, debt restructuring, and offering memoranda for principal investment groups
- Conducted over 20 separate real estate investment services, including in-depth debt restructuring, quantitative financial analyses, and due diligence on 30 deals
- Completed merger and acquisition services on up to seven deals at a time, including 24 private placement and 23 exclusive sales of middle-market companies
- Purchased and placed $125 million in corporate business debt, executing 24 business valuations, including fairness and solvency opinions
- Developed 35 new business opportunities with middle-market companies for purchase and corporate bond reissues

Firewater, Piper and Fink | Los Angeles, CA   2004–2009
Analyst, Restructuring/Litigation Group
- Provided restructuring and bankruptcy advice to 45 creditor corporations, including due diligence and debt restructuring analyses
- Prepared internal financials for 45 client corporations and evaluated alternative strategic plans for 37 restructured companies
- Designed financial models for 36 distressed companies

HONORARY CONSULTING
University of San Francisco | San Francisco, CA   2005–Present
Board of Governors
Proposed $5.6 million in annual savings plan, and established five new student scholarships

EDUCATION
University of San Francisco | San Francisco, CA
Bachelor of Arts, Economics/Philosophy

Functional Résumé

Lucy Superior, RN
312-555-0123
LucySuperior@contactme.com; URL: ContactMe.com/LucySuperior
3232 Pleasant Lane, Chicago, IL

SKILLS
- Conflict and crisis resolution
- Team leader, and total-charge responsibility
- Expert in research and data collection in clinical setting
- Writing for consumer and health care publications

EXPERIENCE
Counseling
- Crisis intervention and long-term counseling with individuals from diverse backgrounds and problems, including confinement, terminal illness, and institutional group living
- Advised 350 study group volunteers of positive test results of venereal disease, TB, high blood pressure, and other abnormal blood values
- Directed and coordinated the medical follow-up for 300 at-risk individuals

Research
- Completed 40 human nutrition research studies
- Established 12 critical test procedures
- Prepared 2,000 samples for analysis and transport

Management/Supervision
- Head nurse in charge of supervising 55 support staff, research volunteers, and graduate students for a Northwestern University nutritional study
- Authored two 80-page procedural manuals and delivered in-service training talks to 300 staff members
- Taught data-collection and handling techniques to 75 research participants
- Assembled data and wrote 42 reports of studies

EMPLOYMENT
2009–Present	**Northwestern University/USDA**
	Research/Clinical Nurse II
2007–2009	**Chicago School District**
	Health Consultant

EDUCATION
- BA, Journalism, DePaul University, Chicago, IL
- RN, Northwestern University, Evanston, IL

Creative Résumé

Alfred G. Newman
777-222-8888
Alfredgnewman@contactme.com URL: SeeMe.com/AlfredGNewman
Eugene, OR

COMPUTER COMPANY SERVICE MANAGER

QUALIFICATIONS
- Diagnosed and repaired computers with a 97 percent accuracy rate
- Skilled in all major computer equipment types
- Experienced in both working independently and supervising others

EXPERIENCE
- Used diagnostic programs to locate defective components on all types of PET computers
- Detected and resolved problems beyond the scope of diagnostic programs, such as thermal integrated circuit failure in keyboard connector
- Maintained 96 percent efficiency in all electronic equipment, including microcomputers

EMPLOYMENT

2006–Present   **University of California, Berkeley,**
                   CAR Astronomy Laboratory
                   Senior Electronics Technician
                   Test and install sensitive receivers and computer-control equipment for radio and optical telescopes, working from engineer sketches and diagrams

2003–2006   **Beckman Instruments, Richmond, CA**
                   Electronics Technician
                   Developed, tested, and repaired prototypes for high-speed electronic counters

EDUCATION
- **Santa Monica City College, Santa Monica, CA**
Engineering major, three-year associate's degree

- **University of California, Berkeley**
Electrical Engineering major, two years

COVER LETTER

The keys are to make it conversational, brief, and to the point. Close by suggesting the next step toward the interview, if possible.

Dear Abigal Overwrought,

John Reason, our mutual friend, suggested I contact you about the senior editor position at Vice News. I've followed your publication with great interest and believe my skills may be the right fit for Vice News. Here's how I think I measure up:

Ad Requirements	My Skills
• Journalism degree	• Graduated cum laude, Northwestern Univ., B.S. in journalism
• 3 to 5 years of editorial experience	• 3½ yrs. as assistant editor at *Squeak*
• Works well under pressure	• Met all deadlines, delivered under budget, and maintained 85% good to excellent reporter relations past 3 yrs.

I'd like to review the details of my qualifications (see résumé) in a personal interview, and will call your office on Wednesday to arrange a convenient time.

Sincerely yours,
Sybil Excels

ALWAYS WRITE A THANK-YOU NOTE

Within twenty-four hours, sit down and handwrite a note of thanks on your personal stationery (notecard) to each person involved in the interview process. Hand-address each envelope. To the individual(s) who interviewed you and will make the hiring decision, very briefly and enthusiastically mention a point that compliments the organization and emphasizes your fit for the position.

FOLLOW UP

How, when, and with whom you follow up will depend on the situation, but try to time follow-up telephone calls and inquiries to best meet the hiring person's timetable. Rehearse your message. Express your enthusiasm and interest, but don't lapse into overeagerness or desperation. And don't place repeated calls and leave a string of telephone messages.

If the hiring process stagnates, offer to supply something additional that could tip the balance in your favor. And don't stop applying for other positions until you are happily employed.

References

American Heritage Dictionary of the English Language. 5th ed. Boston: Houghton Mifflin Harcourt, 2011.

The Associated Press Stylebook and Briefing on Media Law, 2014. Edited by Darrell Christian, Paula Froke, Sally Jacobsen, and David Minthorn. New York: Basic Books, 2014.

Bernstein, Theodore M. *The Careful Writer.* New York: Atheneum/Macmillan, 1965.

The Compact Edition of the Oxford English Dictionary. 2nd ed. New York: Oxford University Press, 1991.

Clark, Roy Peter. *Writing Tools: 50 Essential Strategies for Every Writer.* New York: Little, Brown, 2008.

Fowler, H. W. *Fowler's Modern English Usage.* 2nd ed. Oxford: Oxford University Press, 1965.

Garvey, Mark. *Stylized: A Slightly Obsessive History of Strunk and White's* The Elements of Style. New York: Simon & Schuster, 2009.

Hale, Constance. *Sin and Syntax: How to Craft Wickedly Effective Prose.* Rev. updated ed. New York: Three Rivers Press, 2013.

Huddleston, Rodney, and Geoffrey K. Pullum. *The Cambridge Grammar of the English Language.* New York: Cambridge University Press, 2002.

———. *A Student's Introduction to English Grammar.* New York: Cambridge University Press, 2005.

Lamb, Sandra E. *How to Write It: A Complete Guide to Everything You'll Ever Write.* 3rd ed. Berkeley: Ten Speed Press/Random House, 2011.

Lederer, Richard. *Anguished English: An Anthology of Accidental Assaults on Our Language.* New York: Dell, 1989.

O'Conner, Patricia. *Woe Is I: The Grammarphobe's Guide to Better English in Plain English.* New York: Riverhead Books, 1998.

———. *Words Fail Me: What Everyone Who Writes Should Know About Writing.* New York: Harcourt Brace, 1999.

Pinker, Steven. *The Sense of Style: The Thinking Person's Guide to Writing in the 21st Century.* New York: Penguin, 2014.

Siegal, Allan M., and William G. Connolly. *The New York Times Manual of Style and Usage: The Official Style Guide Used by the Writers and Editors of the World's Most Authoritative Newspaper.* New York: Three Rivers Press, 1999.

Skillin, Marjorie E. and Robert M. Gay. *Words into Type.* Englewood Cliffs, N.J.: Prentice-Hall, Inc., 1974.

Strunk, William, Jr., and E. B. White. *The Elements of Style.* 2nd ed. New York: Macmillan, 1979.

Sword, Helen. *Stylish Academic Writing.* Cambridge, Mass.: Harvard University Press, 2012.

Thomas, Francis-Noel, and Mark Turner. *Clear and Simple as the Truth: Writing Classic Prose.* 2nd ed. Princeton, N.J.: Princeton University Press, 2011.

Truss, Lynne. *Eats, Shoots and Leaves: The Zero Tolerance Approach to Punctuation.* New York: Gotham Books, 2003.

University of Chicago Press. *The Chicago Manual of Style.* 16th ed. Chicago: University of Chicago Press, 2010.

Walsh, Bill. *The Elephants of Style: A Trunkload of Tips on the Big Issues and Gray Areas of Contemporary American English.* New York: McGraw-Hill, 2004.

Williams, Joseph M. *Style: Toward Clarity and Grace.* Chicago: University of Chicago Press, 1995.

Zinsser, William. *On Writing Well: The Classic Guide to Writing Nonfiction.* New York: HarperCollins, 1976.

Index

a, an, 106
abbreviations, 75
about, anywhere from, 109–10
about, at about, 106
absolute adjectives, 99
abundant, fulsome, full, 117
abused, misused, and confused words,
   106–25
academic degrees, 75
accept, except, 107
acceptance letters, 173
accident reports, 195–98
action plan, 188
action (active) verbs, 5, 20, 21, 22, 23, 30, 35
active voice, 9–11, 21–25, 35–37, 87
activity (progress) reports, 156, 194
acute, chronic, 107
adapt, adopt, 107
addresses, 84
addressing reader directly, 87–88
adjectival phrases, 80
adjectives, 30, 72, 96–97
   absolute, 99
   comparative, 99–100
   coordinate, 83
   hyphens between nouns and, 80
   nouns and, 83, 84
   placement of, 96
   positive, 99–100
   superlative, 99–100
adopt, adapt, 107
adverbs, 53–54, 56, 96–97
   comparative, 99–100
   conjunctive, 73, 77
   positive, 99–100
   splitting infinitives and, 89
   superlative, 99–100
adverse, averse, 107
advice, advise, 107
affect, effect, 107
affective, effective, 107
afterward, toward, anyway, 124
aggravate, annoy, 108

aid, aide, 108
aisle, isle, 118
Alicia Patterson Award, 206–8
allot, alot, a lot, 108
all ready, already, 108
all right, alright, 108
all together, altogether, 108
allude, elude, 108
allusion, illusion, 108
a lot, alot, allot, 108
alphanumeric outline, 15–16
already, all ready, 108
alright, all right, 108
altar, alter, 108
alternate, alternative, 108
alternatives:
   false dilemma and, 101
   indicating, 81
altogether, all together, 108
alumni, alumnae, alumnus, alum, alumna,
   109
ambiguous comparisons, 99
ambiguous pronouns, 91
am not, do not, is not, cannot, 112
among, between, 109
amused, bemused, 111
an, a, 106
and, 77, 83
and I, and me, 109
anemic words, 27, 38
annoy, aggravate, 108
annual reports, 198–202
antecedents, 91
antennas, antennae, 109
anticipate, expect, 109
anticlimactic, anti-climactic, 109
anybody, any body, 109
anymore, any more, 109
anyway, afterward, toward, 124
anywhere from, about, 109–10
apology letters:
   from offender, 173–74
   requesting apology, 174

appendixes, 188
applicant tracking system (ATS), 222–23, 226, 231
appositives, 94
appraise, apprise, 110
Architectural Digest, 70
as, like, 110
as, pronoun after, 91–92
as good, as to whether, as yet, 110
Aspen Ideas Festival, 32
as per, per, per se, 120
as regards, in regards to, in regard to, 118
as soon as, will, 110
assume, presume, 110
assure, ensure, insure, 110
at about, about, 106
Atlantic, 70
at no charge, free, for free, 116
attorneys, lawyers, 111
audience, 6–7, 45, 65, 70
    addressing directly, 87–88
    attitude about subject, 13
    business plans and, 183–84
    email and, 144
    focusing on, 6–7
    jargon and, 41–42
    knowledge of, about subject, 13, 46, 65
    point of view of, 46
    presentations and, 212–13
    reports and, 190
    tone and, 72, 144–45
averse, adverse, 107

bad, badly, 111
bad news:
    in emails, 156–57
    in letters, 164–65
    rules for giving, 164
banks, 184
bare, bear, 111
because of, due to, 111
Behind the Beautiful Forevers (Boo), 39, 40
bemused, amused, 111
besides, beside, 111
best, ultimate, 124
between, among, 109
Bible, 126
bibliographic listings, 78

board of directors report, 6, 9, 13
    topic sentence for first paragraph of, 10–11
bob and weave, 71
boldface, 44
Bolles, Richard, 225
Boo, Katherine, 39, 40
book titles, 78
both agree, they agree, 111
brackets, 74, 79
brain, 31
brainstorming, 31, 32–33
    for business plans, 185–86
    for proposals and grant applications, 205
    for résumés, 225
breath, breathe, 111
breather, taking, 48, 64
Bush, George H. W., 127–28
business plans, 45, 183–89
    action plan in, 188
    appendixes in, 188
    audience and, 183–84
    banks and, 184
    brainstorming and research for, 185–86
    executive summary/business description in, 186
    financial analysis in, 188
    management team in, 187
    market analysis in, 187
    marketing plan in, 188
    mission statement in, 187
    and need for product, 186
    objectives/goals in, 187
    purpose and, 184
    sales figures in, 186
    strategies in, 187
    tips for, 189
    vision statement in, 186
    what to include in, 184–85
but, 77, 83
buzzwords, 42–43
    top offenders, 58–63

cadence and rhythm, 70, 72, 74
can, may, 112
cannot, am not, do not, is not, 112
capital, capitol, 112

capitalization in emails, 146
carat, caret, carrot, karat, 112
Carroll, Lewis, 129
Carter, Jimmy, 88
caudate nucleus, 31
cause-and-effect relationship, 153
cellphone, cell phone, 112
checklist for corrections, 53
Chief Illiniwek, 127
chronic, acute, 107
chronological order, 153
Churchill, Winston, 219
Cicero, 19
circular reasoning, 101–2
cite, sight, site, 112
cities, countries, and states, 113
    abbreviations for, 75
clarity, 9–11, 18, 19, 20, 21, 30, 35–37, 40,
    50, 63, 89
Clark, Roy Peter, 20, 21, 37, 168
clauses:
    dependent, 74, 91
    independent, 73, 74, 76–77, 83
    independent, faulty coordination
        and, 98
    introductory, 83
clear writing, 9–11, 18, 19, 20, 21, 30,
    35–37, 40, 50, 63, 89
client needs:
    in presentations, 213–14, 215
    in proposals and grant applications,
        205, 209–10
Clinton, Bill, 88
coarse, course, 112
collaborative groups, 148
collection letters, 174–75
collective nouns, 90
colloquial style, 74
colons, 78–79, 81, 85
commas, 73, 76, 77, 79, 82–84, 85
comma splices (comma faults), 104
company names, 91
comparative adjectives and adverbs,
    99–100
comparisons:
    ambiguous, 99
    faulty, 99
    in memos, 153

complaint letters, 175–76
complement, compliment, 112
complements, subject, 94–95
complete sentences, 86
complex ideas, 29
complex sentences, 74
    compound, 74
compliment, complement, 112
composed of, divided into, 114
compound modifiers, 80
compound sentences, 73
    complex, 74
concise writing, 20, 21
    in reports, 191
conclusion, 44
condolence letters, 176–77
confidence:
    in proposals and grant applications,
        209
    about writing skills, 33–34
confused, abused, and misused words,
    106–25
conjunctions:
    beginning sentences with, 87
    coordinating, 73, 76–77, 83, 104
conjunctive adverbs, 73, 77
continued, postponed, 113
contractions, 88
contracts:
    letters of, 177
    requests for, in presentations, 216–17
conversational tone, 9, 29, 40, 41–43,
    49, 65
    in emails, 144–45
coordinate adjectives, 83
coordinating conjunctions, 73, 76–77,
    83, 104
coordination, faulty, 98
copyrights, 142, 148
corporate histories, 45
Cosell, Howard, 127
could of, could have, 113
council, counsel, 113
countries, states, and cities, 113
    abbreviations for, 75
course, coarse, 112
cover letters, 177–78
    for résumés, 231–32, 240

creativity, 31, 32, 33
cure-all, panacea, 120

dashes, 79, 81
data is, data are, 113
dates, 81, 84
deadlines, 32
declarative sentences, 73, 87
deduction, 153
definite, definitive, 113
definition, in memos, 153
defuse, diffuse, 113
degrees, academic, 75
dependent clauses, 74, 91
dessert, desert, 113
details, 168
Dickens, Charles, 77, 82
different from, different than, 113
diffuse, defuse, 113
dilemma, 114
direct address, 84
disassemble, dissemble, 114
disburse, disperse, 114
discipline, 32
discreet, discrete, 114
disinterested, indifferent, uninterested,
    114
disperse, disburse, 114
dissemble, disassemble, 114
distractions, 33
divided into, composed of, 114
division and classification, 153
do not, am not, is not, cannot, 112
drafts, 45, 47
    email, 145
    first (rough), 34, 45, 46, 71, 73
dual, duel, 114
due to, because of, 111

each and every, every one, everyone, 114
editing, 11–12, 48–65
    of emails, 142–43, 145
    final, 53–64
editors, letters to, 178–79
effect, affect, 107
effective, affective, 107
e.g., i.e., 118
Egypt, 126

eighth-grade level, writing to, 88
Elements of Style, The (Strunk and White),
    1, 11, 21, 50
Elephants of Style, The (Walsh), 69, 88
elimination, 46
Eliot, George, 39
ellipses, 82
elude, allude, 108
email, 1, 2, 3–4, 137–51
    adding value to, 5–6, 144
    advantages of, 137, 141
    alternatives to, 139–43
    attachments to, 143
    collaboration and, 148
    copyright and, 142, 148
    drafts of, 145
    editing of, 142–43, 145
    effective, 143–45
    etiquette and, 139, 147–48, 150–51
    face-to-face communication vs.,
        139–40
    faxes vs., 141
    flaming, 148
    forwarding of, 142
    inappropriate, 142
    instant messaging vs., 143
    as interruption, 142
    and knowing your reader, 144
    letters vs., 140
    memos and, 137, 152
    organizing content for, 144
    problems presented by, 138, 142–43
    proofreading of, 145
    purpose in, 144
    rules for, 139–43, 149
    salutations in, 146
    as searchable records, 142
    sentence fragments in, 102
    signature blocks on, 146–47
    snark in, 129
    subject line of, 145–46
    telephone vs., 137, 140
    texting vs., 143
    tips for, 149–50
    TO, CC, REPLY ALL, and BCC in, 147
    tone in, 142, 144–45, 148
    unnecessary, 137–38, 142
    vacations and, 151

emigrate, immigrate, 114
emotional messages, 139, 140, 148
empty phrases, 35
ensure, insure, assure, 110
enthusiasm, in proposals and grant
    applications, 209
envelop, envelope, 115
envelopes, 168
era designations, 75
etiquette, 126–33
    email and, 139, 147–48, 150–51
    gender terms and, 130–31
    labels and, 130
    netiquette, 139, 147–48
    origin of word, 126
    political correctness and, 127–19, 130,
        131
    snark and, 129–30
    tips for, 132–33
*Etiquette in Society, in Business, in Politics
    and at Home* (Post), 127
everyday, every day, 115
every one, everyone, each and every,
    114
exact words, 38–40
except, accept, 107
exceptions to the rule, 73, 86
exclamation points, 76
executive summaries, 44, 186
expect, anticipate, 109
expedient, expeditious, 115
expense reports, 195

face-to-face communication, 139–40
facts, 17, 32, 33
    adding, 46
    checking, 46
    in reports, 191
false (fallacious) dilemma, 101
farther, further, 115
faulty comparisons, 99
faulty coordination, 98
faulty predication, 98
faxes, 141
faze, phase, 115
feasibility reports, 194
fewer, less, 115
Fighting Chance, A (Warren), 40, 41

final edit, 53–64
financial analysis, 188
first (rough) draft, 34, 45, 46, 71, 73
first paragraph, lead or topic sentence for,
    10–11
first person, 70–71, 87, 93
flammable, inflammable, 115
flaunt, flout, 116
flesh, flush, 116
flounder, founder, 116
flow, writing in, 11, 34
flush, flesh, 116
focus, 14
focusing on your reader, 6–7
fog count, 88
folk, folks, 116
for, 77, 83
Forbes, 223, 234
forego, forgo, foregone, 116
foreword, forward, 116
for example, 77
for free, free, at no charge, 116
formal tone, 72
fortuitous, fortunate, 116
forward, foreword, 116
forward slants, 81–82
founder, flounder, 116
Franklin, Benjamin, 126
free, for free, at no charge, 116
Friedman, Thomas, 70
fulsome, full, abundant, 117
fund-raising letters, 178
further, farther, 115
fused sentences, 103

gauge, gage, 117
gay, homosexual, 117
Gehrig, Lou, 219
gender terms, 130–31
general or vague words and phrases,
    26–27, 38, 51, 100
gerunds, 24, 58, 95
glance over, peruse, 121
goals, business, 187
Golden Rule, 126
    in résumés, 226
good, well, 117
good news, 163

grammar rules, 86–105
  discredited, 86–89
  exceptions to, 73, 86
  to write by, 89–105
grant applications, 45, 203–11
  call for action in, 210
  confidence in, 209
  enthusiasm in, 209
  keeping to the point in, 209–10
  outline in, 208
  pizzazz in, 211
  problem and solution in, 205, 209–10
  Q&A in, 210
  research for, 203, 204–5
  RFPs (request for proposals) and, 44,
    203, 204, 208, 210
  strong finish in, 210
  thinking through, 205–8
gratuitous, gratitude, grateful, 117

Hale, Constance, 144
handwritten notes, 140
heads and subheads, 33, 44
  in presentations, 215–16
hear, here, 117
hedging, 38, 56, 71
Hemingway, Ernest, 19
here, hear, 117
"he said," 84
hoard, horde, 117
homosexual, gay, 117
honesty, 17
hopefully, I hope, it is hoped, 117–18
horde, hoard, 117
hot writing, 32
however, 77
How to Write It (Lamb), 16, 27–28, 49,
  225
How to Write Short (Clark), 21
human resources departments (HR),
  224, 231, 232
"Hunting of the Snark, The" (Carroll),
  129
hyphens, 80–81

I, me, myself, 119
i.e., e.g., 118
I hope, it is hoped, hopefully, 117–18

illusion, allusion, 108
imitation, 71
immigrate, emigrate, 114
imperative sentences, 73
imply, infer, 118
importance, order of, 153
in, into, 118
in, within, 125
in box, in-box, inbox, 118
incident reports, 195–98
incomplete sentences, 74
indefinite pronouns, 90
independent clauses, 73, 74, 76–77, 83
  faulty coordination and, 98
indifferent, uninterested, disinterested,
  114
induction, 153
in fact, 77
infer, imply, 118
infinitives, 95, 96
  splitting, 88–89, 96
inflammable, flammable, 115
in regard to, as regards, in regards to,
  118
instant messaging (IM), 143
insure, assure, ensure, 110
interjections, 84
Internet, 112
  etiquette and, 129, 130
interrogative tags, 84
into, in, 118
introductory clauses, 83
inverted sentences, 90
investigative reports, 195
irregardless, regardless, 118
isle, aisle, 118
is not, am not, do not, cannot, 112
items in a series, 76
it is hoped, I hope, hopefully, 117–18
its, it's, 118

jargon, 26, 30, 41–42
  top offenders, 58–63
Jimmy the Greek, 127
job applications:
  follow up and, 241
  human resources departments and,
    224, 231, 232

immediate response to openings, 231
networking and, 224
résumés in, *see* résumés
thank-you notes and, 240–41
Joint Commission, 47

karat, carat, caret, carrot, 112
kill your darlings, 48

labels, 130
Lapsing Into a Comma (Walsh), 25
lawyers, attorneys, 111
lay, lie, 118–19
lead, led, 119
lead sentence for first paragraph, 10–11
led, lead, 119
legal documents, 140
lend, loan, 119
Leonard, Elmore, 48
less, fewer, 115
letters, 158–82
    acceptance, 173
    additional pages of, 172
    apology (from the offender), 173–74
    apology (requesting), 174
    attachments or enclosures with,
        171
    bad news in, 164–65
    body of, 169
    closing paragraph of, 169–70
    collection, 174–75
    complaint, 175–76
    condolence/sympathy, 176–77
    contract, 177
    cover, 177–78
    cover, for résumés, 231–32, 240
    to customer, 71
    to editor, 178–79
    emails vs., 140
    end notations in, 171
    envelopes for, 168
    format and form for, 168–72
    fund-raising, 178
    good news in, 163
    inside address in, 168
    language and tone in, 158–60
    negotiation, 179–80
    pitch, 180–81

refusal, 181
request, 181
salutation in, 78, 168–69
settlement, 181–82
signature in, 170–71
signature block in, 171
sincerity in, 160–63
structure of, 165–67
subject line of, 169
tips for, 173–82
levee, levy, 119
Levy, Builder, 207
lie, lay, 118–19
like, as, 110
linear sequence, 16
linking verbs, 21–22, 23
loan, lend, 119
logic:
    non sequiturs and, 101
    of sentences, 98
long-standing, longtime, 119
loose, lose, 119
Lotze, Martin, 31
Louis XIV, King, 126
-ly words, 53–54, 96, 97

MacArthur, Douglas, 219
management team, 187
M&C Saatchi, 18
market analysis, 187
marketing plan, 188
Mason, Jackie, 127
may, can, 112
me, myself, I, 119
meaning, 25–26
meeting agendas, 155
meeting announcements, 155
memos, 152–57
    bad news, 156–57
    checking for completeness, 154
    emails and, 137, 152
    general requirements for, 155
    meeting agendas, 155
    meeting announcements, 155
    personnel- or organizational-change
        announcements, 156
    policy and procedure changes, 157
    progress reports, 156

memos *(continued)*
  recommendations, 157
  structure of, 152–54
  tips for, 155–57
message statements, 7–8, 10, 18, 32, 33,
    43, 45
  examples of, 19–20
Middle Ages, 126
Middlemarch (Eliot), 39
militate, mitigate, 119
mind mapping, 15
mission statements, 187
misused, confused, and abused words,
    106–25
mitigate, militate, 119
modifiers, 49, 89
  compound, 80
  and keeping related words together,
    40, 63
mould, mold, 119
muddy thinking, 18, 33, 34
muddy writing, examples of, 35–37
multisyllable words, 41, 42, 72, 88
multitasking, 33
myself, me, I, 119

natural, conversational tone, 9, 29, 40,
    41–43, 49, 65
  in emails, 144
needless words and phrases, 49–50
needs clients:
  in presentations, 213–14, 215
  in proposals and grant applications,
    205, 209–10
negotiation, 139, 140
  letters of, 179–80
netiquette, 139, 147–48
  see also etiquette
networking, 224
Newsday, 206
New Yorker, 70
New York Times, 20, 31, 127, 128, 146
"no," 84
nominalizations, 23–24, 30
non sequiturs, 101
nor, 77, 83
notable, notorious, 120
notes, 32, 34

notorious, notable, 120
nouns, 58
  adjectives and, 83, 84
  ambiguous pronouns and, 91
  appositives and, 94
  collective, 90
  gerunds and, 24
  hyphens between adjectives and, 80
  nominalizations and, 23–24, 30
  plural, 89–91
  singular, 89–91
novelty words, 30
numbers, 80–81
numeral dates, 81

objective pronouns, 93, 105
objectives, business, 187
objectivity, 17
obscurity, 38, 50, 51–53
O'Conner, Patricia, 34
official documents, 140
Official Politically Correct Dictionary, The
    (Beard and Cerf), 128–29
on line, online, 120
On Writing Well (Zinsser), 1, 5, 9, 16–17,
    21, 37, 45, 46, 70, 71
opaque language, 38, 50, 51–53
options, indicating, 81
or, 77, 83
organizational-change announcements,
    156
organization names, 75
organizing, 8–9, 13–14
  email and, 144
  presentations and, 214
  reorganizing, 46
or more, up to, 124
outlines, 14–16, 33–34, 46
  alphanumerical, 15–16
  for proposals and grant applications,
    208

pallet, palate, palette, 120
panacea, cure-all, 120
papers, titles of, 78
paragraphs:
  short, 43
  topic sentences in, 10–11, 43

parentheses, 74, 79
parenthetical phrases, 40, 81, 83
participles, 95
Pascal, Blaise, 19
passed, surpassed, past, 120
passive verbs, 21, 22
passive voice, 22–23, 87
past, passed, surpassed, 120
Patterson, Alicia, 206
peak, peek, pique, 120
Penn, William, 126
per, as per, per se, 120
peremptory, preemptive, 120
periods, 73–75, 76
perpetrate, perpetuate, 120
perquisite, prerequisite, 121
person, grammatical:
   consistent, 93–94
   first, 70–71, 87, 93
   second, 93
   third, 71, 93
personal approach, in speeches, 219
personal messages, 139, 140
personal titles, 75, 84
personnel issues, 139, 140
   memos and, 156
perspective, prospective, 121
persuasive writing, 183, 203
peruse, glance over, 121
phase, faze, 115
photogenic, photographic, 121
phrases:
   adjectival, 80
   empty, 35
   needless, 49–50
   nonrestrictive and restrictive, 83
   parenthetical, 40, 81, 83
   prepositional, 36, 54–55
   transitional, 78
   useless, 55–56
   vague, 26–27, 38
pique, peak, peek, 120
pitch letters, 180–81
pizzazz:
   in presentations, 216
   in proposals and grant applications, 211
plagiarism and copyright, 142, 148

pleaded, pled, 121
poetry, 82
Polgreen, Lydia, 20
policy changes, 157
political correctness, 127–19, 130, 131
pomposity, 35
pore, pour, 121
positive adjectives and adverbs, 99–100
possessive pronouns, 93, 105
Post, Emily, 127
postponed, continued, 113
pour, pore, 121
PowerPoint, power point, Powerpoint, 121
practice, 31
   of delivering speech, 220
practice, practise, 121
precede, proceed, 121
precise writing, 25–28, 30, 38, 42
predication, faulty, 98
preemptive, peremptory, 120
prepositional phrases, 36, 54–55
prepositions, ending sentences with, 87
prerequisite, perquisite, 121
prescribe, proscribe, 121
presentations, 212–17
   audience for, 212–13
   client's problem or need in, 213–14, 215
   contract request in, 216–17
   gimmicks and giveaways in, 216
   heads and subheads in, 215–16
   laying out plan of, 214
   organizing, 214
   pizzazz in, 216
   professionalism in, 215–16
   Q&A segment of, 214, 216
   staying on target in, 214–15
   taking control in, 213
   "you" focus in, 215
presume, assume, 110
prevaricate, procrastinate, 122
principle, principal, 122
printing, 49
problem and needs of clients:
   in presentations, 213–14, 215
   in proposals and grant applications, 205, 209–10

procedure changes, 157
proceed, precede, 121
procrastinate, prevaricate, 122
Procter & Gamble, 231
progeny, prodigy, 122
progress reports, 156, 194
pronouns, 63, 105
  ambiguous, 91
  appositives and, 94
  gender and, 130–31
  indefinite, 90
  objective, 93, 105
  personal, cases of, 105
  possessive, 93, 105
  relative, 91
  subjective, 93, 94–95, 105
  after *than* or *as,* 91–92
proofreading emails, 145
proper nouns ending in *y,* 124
proportions, 78
proposals, 45, 203–11
  call for action in, 210
  confidence in, 209
  enthusiasm in, 209
  keeping to the point in, 209–10
  outline in, 208
  pizzazz in, 211
  problem and solution in, 205, 209–10
  Q&A in, 210
  research for, 203, 204–5
  RFPs (request for proposals) and, 44, 203, 204, 208, 210
  strong finish in, 210
  thinking through, 205–8
proscribe, prescribe, 121
prospective, perspective, 121
punctuation, 73–85
  brackets, 74, 79
  colons, 78–79, 81, 85
  commas, 73, 76, 77, 79, 82–84, 85
  dashes, 79, 81
  ellipses, 82
  exclamation points, 76
  hyphens, 80–81
  mistakes to avoid in, 85
  parentheses, 74, 79
  periods, 73–75, 76
  question marks, 76

semicolons, 73, 76–78, 85
  slashes, 81–82
purpose, 7, 13, 70
  in business plans, 184
  in emails, 144
  in reports, 191

qualifiers, 56–58
question marks, 76
quite, quiet, 122
quotations, 82, 84

rain, rein, reign, 122
reader, 6–7, 45, 65, 70
  addressing directly, 87–88
  attitude about subject, 13
  business plans and, 183–84
  email and, 144
  focusing on, 6–7
  jargon and, 41–42
  knowledge of, about subject, 13, 46, 65
  point of view of, 46
  presentations and, 212–13
  reports and, 190
  tone and, 72, 144–45
reading aloud, 9, 12, 29, 49, 65, 69–70, 71, 72
reading good writers, 70, 71, 72
Reagan, Ronald, 219
real, really, 122
recommendations:
  memos, 157
  reports, 194
recording facts, 17
red herrings, 102
refusal letters, 181
regardless, irregardless, 118
rein, reign, rain, 122
related words, keeping together, 40–41, 63
relative pronouns, 91
reluctant, reticent, 122
reorganizing, 46
repair reports, 194–95
repetition, 49, 54–55
reports, 45, 190–202
  annual, 198–202
  audience and, 190

back material in, 193
to board of directors, 6, 9, 10–11, 13
body of, 192–93
concise language in, 191
expense, 195
facts in, 191
feasibility (recommendation), 194
format for, 191–93
front material in, 192
investigative, 195
organizing, 14
progress (activity), 156, 194
purpose in, 191
to research team, 6, 8–9, 10, 13
scope and budget in, 201
steps to follow in, 190–91
structure of, 191, 201–2
thoroughness in, 191
trip (repair; service), 194–95
trouble (accident; incident), 195–98
types of, 194–202
request for proposals (RFPs), 44, 203,
    204, 208, 210
request letters, 181
rereading, 45, 46
research, 16–17, 25–26, 32
    for annual reports, 200
    for business plans, 185–86
    linear sequence in, 16
    for proposals and grant applications,
       203, 204–5
    sources for, 17
research team report, 6, 8–9, 13
    topic sentence for first paragraph of,
       10
résumés, 222–41
    applicant tracking system (ATS) and,
       222–23, 226, 231
    and applying for position immediately,
       231
    brainstorming for, 225
    chronological, 226, 236–37
    cover letter for, 231–32, 240
    creative, 226, 239
    developing, 225–26
    examples of, 236–39
    examples of category entries in, 233–34
    experience in, 226, 228–29

expert example of, 234–35
final, building, 226–30
follow up and, 241
format for, 227
functional, 226, 238
and giving yourself the best chance,
    223–24
and going with your strengths,
    224–25
honesty in, 226
objective/executive summary in, 226,
    228
online applications and, 222–23
optional sections in, 229–30
taking a last, critical look at, 230
thank-you note and, 240–41
top material in, 228
reticent, reluctant, 122
reviewers, 47
revising and rewriting, 45–47, 48
    see also editing
RFPs (request for proposals), 44, 203,
    204, 208, 210
rhythm and cadence, 70, 72, 74
right-branching sentences, 20
road map, 13–17, 34
Rometty, Virginia M., 200, 234–35
Roosevelt, Eleanor, 218
Roosevelt, Franklin D., 27
rough (first) draft, 34, 45, 46, 71, 73
run-on sentences, 73, 103–5

Safire, William, 128
St. Petersburg Times, 168
Saint-Simon, Louis de Rouvroy, duc de,
    126
salutations:
    in emails, 146
    in letters, 78, 168–69
sat, set, sit, 122–23
second person, 93
Sellers, Frances Stead, 208
semicolons, 73, 76–78, 85
sentence fragments, 102–3
sentences:
    beginning with a conjunction, 87
    complete, 86
    complex, 74

sentences *(continued)*
  compound, 73
  compound complex, 74
  contorted, 50–51
  declarative, 73, 87
  front-loading, 36
  fused, 103
  imperative, 73
  incomplete, 74
  inverted, 90
  length of, 72
  logic of, 98
  reducing to simplest form, 105
  right-branching, 20
  run-on, 73, 103–5
  separating subject and verb in, 37
  short, 19–21, 37–38, 51–53
  simple, clear, 50–51
  structure of, 36–37
  topic, 10–11, 43
sequential order, 153
serial commas, 84
series, 76
service reports, 194–95
set, sit, sat, 122–23
settlement letters, 181–82
setup statement, 32
sexism, 130
"she said," 84
Shevory, Kristina, 207
short writing, 19–21
  paragraphs, 43
  sentences, 19–21, 37–38, 51–53
[*sic*], 79
sight, site, cite, 112
signature blocks:
  in emails, 146–47
  in letters, 171
signatures:
  in letters, 170–71
  requirements for, 140, 141
simple words and ideas, 9–11, 18, 34–35,
    50–51
  examples of, 27–28, 35–37
  using the simplest words, 88
Sin and Syntax (Hale), 144
sincerity, 160–63
sit, set, sat, 122–23

site, cite, sight, 112
skills, 31
slashes, 81–82
snark, 129–30
so, 77, 83
sources, 17
spatial development, 153
specific words, 38–40
speeches, 49, 218–21
  ending on high note, 221
  leaping into, 220
  personal approach in, 219
  pizzazz in, 219
  practicing, 220
  theme, subject, and title for, 218–19
sports terms, 63
states, countries, and cities, 113
  abbreviations for, 75
stationery, stationary, 123
strategies, business, 187
streamlining, 29
stream of consciousness, 15
strong words, 27, 38–40
Strunk, William, Jr., 1, 11, 18, 21, 50,
    53–54, 71
stuffy language, 9, 29
style, 69–72
  colloquial, 74
  see also tone; voice
subheads, 33, 44
  in presentations, 215–16
subject complements, 94–95
subjective pronouns, 93, 94–95, 105
subject lines:
  of emails, 145–46
  of letters, 169
subject of speech, 218–19
subjects, grammatical, 20, 35
  agreement of verb and, 89–91
  complete sentences and, 86
  compound, 89
  faulty predication and, 98
  front-loading sentence with, 36
  and keeping related words together,
    40, 63
  plural, 89–90
  separating verb and, 37
  singular, 89–90

subordinate (dependent) clauses, 74, 91
summaries, 44
  executive, 44
Summers, Larry, 128
superlatives, 99–100
supposed to, suppose to, 123
surpassed, passed, past, 120
syllables, 41, 42, 72, 88
sympathy letters, 176–77

tack, tact, 123
Tale of Two Cities, A (Dickens), 77, 82
Talk to the Hand (Truss), 128
Talmud, 126
telephone, 137, 140
texting, 143
than, pronoun after, 91–92
than, then, 123
thank-you notes, 240–41
that, 91
that, which, 123
their, they're, there, 123
TheLadders, 225
theme, of speech, 218–19
then, than, 123
there, their, they're, 123
they agree, both agree, 111
they're, there, their, 123
third person, 71, 93
till, til, 123
time, setting aside for writing, 33
time designations, 75, 78
titles:
  of books and papers, 78
  plural nouns in, 91
  of speeches, 218–19
titles, personal, 75, 84
to, too, two, 123
to be verbs, 22, 23, 30
tone, 38–40, 69–72
  checking, 46, 49
  conversational, 9, 29, 40, 41–43, 49,
    65, 144
  in emails, 142, 144–45, 148
  formal, 72
  in letters, 158–60
  see also voice
too, two, to, 123

topic sentences, 10–11, 43
toward, anyway, afterward, 124
transitional phrases, 78
treasurys, treasuries, 124
trip reports, 194–95
troop, troupe, 124
trouble reports, 195–98
Truss, Lynne, 128
try and, try to, 124
Twain, Mark, 19, 50
two, to, too, 123

ultimate, best, 124
underlining, 44
uninterested, disinterested, indifferent, 114
University of Griefswald, 31
up to, or more, 124
useless phrases, 55–56
use to, used to, 124
U.S. News & World Report, 70

vacations, and email, 151
vague or general words and phrases,
    26–27, 38, 51, 100
value, adding, 34–35
  to emails, 5–6, 144
van der Voo, Lee, 207
verbs, 21, 36–37, 58
  action (active), 5, 20, 21, 22, 23, 30, 35
  adverbs and, 54
  agreement of subject and, 89–91
  anemic, 27
  complete sentences and, 86
  faulty predication and, 98
  forms of, 95–96
  front-loading sentence with, 36
  gerunds, 24, 58, 95
  infinitives, 95, 96
  infinitives, splitting, 88–89, 96
  and keeping related words together,
    40, 63
  linking, 21–22, 23
  nominalizations and, 23–24, 30
  participles, 95
  passive, 21, 22
  plural, 89–91
  separating subject and, 37
  singular, 89–91

verbs *(continued)*
  strong and precise, 27
  tenses of, 63
  to be, 22, 23, 30
  vivid, 26, 27
vision statements, 186
voice, 69–72
  conversational, 9, 29, 40, 41–43, 49, 65
  see also tone
voice, grammatical:
  active, 9–11, 21–25, 35–37, 87
  passive, 22–23, 87
Voltaire, 19

waffle words, 56, 71
Wall Street Journal, 42
Walsh, Bill, 25, 69, 88
warrantee, warranty, 124
Warren, Elizabeth, 40, 41
Washington, George, 126
Washington Post, 88
weak language, 38, 57–58
weasel words, 38, 71
well, good, 117
What Color Is Your Parachute? (Bolles),
  225
which, 91
which, that, 123
White, E. B., 1, 21
who, 91
  whom vs., 92–93, 124
whose, who's, 124
wiggle (waffle) words, 56, 71
will, as soon as, 110
Will, George, 70
within, in, 125
Woe Is I (O'Conner), 34

writing, 31–44
  active voice in, 9–11, 21–25, 35–37
  from beginning to end, 34
  brain scans and, 31
  brainstorming and, 31, 32–33
  clear, 9–11, 18, 19, 20, 21, 30, 35–37,
    40, 50, 63
  concise, 20, 21, 191
  conversational tone in, 9, 29, 40,
    41–43, 49, 65, 144
  exact, specific, strong words and right
    tone in, 38–40
  in the flow, 11, 34
  giving yourself the assignment for, 32
  heads and subheads in, 33, 44
  hot, 32
  keeping related words together in,
    40–41, 63
  notes and, 32, 34
  precise, 25–28, 30, 38, 42
  setting aside time for, 33
  short, 19–21, 37–38, 44
  short paragraphs in, 43
  summary in, 44
  topic sentences in, 10–11, 43
  voice in, 9, 29
  the way you speak, 5, 9
  well, expectation of, 33–34
Writing Tools (Clark), 20, 37, 168

"yes," 84
yet, 77, 83
your, you're, 125

Zimmer, Carl, 31
Zinsser, William, 1, 5, 9, 16–17, 21, 37,
  45, 46, 70, 71